Terence Davies was born in Liverpoo[...] [...]
ten children, of whom seven survived [...]
was based loosely on his experiences [...]
Catholic Boys' School, which he left [...]
became an articled clerk, and then w[...]
accountant and book-keeper for twelve years in an office opposite
Liverpool's internationally famous Cavern Club, which he never
visited. He joined a writers' club and became an amateur actor. In
1972 Terence Davies went to Coventry Drama School, where he
wrote *Children*, which was produced by the British Film Institute
and won the Bronze Hugo at the Chicago Film Festival in 1983.
He went on to the National Film School where he shot *Madonna
and Child*, winner of the Golden Hugo. His third film, *Death and
Transfiguration*, was made after leaving film school with funding
from the Greater London Arts Association and the British Film
Institute.

This trilogy of films went on to win several European prizes. In
1984 Davies published a novel, *Hallelujah Now*. His next two
films, completed in 1988, were released as *Distant Voices, Still
Lives* and introduced Davies's work to an international audience
when they won the International Critics Prize at Cannes, 1988.
The Long Day Closes (1992) has been selected for competition at
Cannes and marks the final work in Davies's autobiographical
cycle of films.

Photo by Sarah Fitzgerald

A Modest Pageant

*Children, Madonna and Child,
Death and Transfiguration, Distant Voices,
Still Lives and The Long Day Closes*

Six Screenplays with an Introduction

TERENCE DAVIES

faber and faber
LONDON · BOSTON

First published in 1992
by Faber and Faber Limited
3 Queen Square London WCIN 3AU

Photoset by Parker Typesetting Service, Leicester
Printed in England by Clays Ltd, St Ives plc

Photographs reproduced by courtesy of
Sarah Fitzgerald and Tom Hilton

British Library Cataloguing in Publication Data is available

ISBN 0–571–16371–8

For my Mother

CONTENTS

INTRODUCTION

Looking back over these texts, which represent my entire output over a period of eighteen years, has been a strange experience for me.

The reason I began making films came from a deep *need* to do so in order to come to terms with my family's history and suffering, to make sense of the past and to explore my own personal terrors, both mental and spiritual, and to examine the destructive nature of Catholicism. Film as an expression of guilt, film as confession (psychotherapy would be much cheaper but a lot less fun).

My earliest influences, however, couldn't have been more jolly, couldn't have been less grim: the American musical, the British comedy, Gene Kelly, Judy Garland, Danny Kaye, Margaret Rutherford, Alistair Sim, Terry-Thomas, Joyce Grenfell and – above all – Doris Day. To see *Young at Heart* in those wonderfully glowing colours was like experiencing life itself in three-strip Technicolor. *Singin' in the Rain*, *White Christmas*, *Kind Hearts and Coronets*, *The Happiest Days of Your Life* and *The Ladykillers* – these films made my childhood in the Liverpool of the 1950s seem enchanted.

It seemed as if these riches were endless. Little did we understand 'the studio system', nor have any inkling of its imminent collapse. America was the Land of Magic, England the Land of Comedy. They say that the greatest monuments to an age are constructed at the close of that age and it was thus in my childhood. Such glories! All gone, alas.

But those films have stayed with me. Though at first glance the reader and viewer may find very little Technicolor magic or laughs in my work, if you look closely however you will just perceive those influences, tentative at first, but gradually increasing in prominence as the works progress. Doris Day singing 'It All Depends on You' at the opening of the final part of the trilogy *Death and Transfiguration*, through to 'Love is a Many-Splendoured Thing' in the cinema sequence of *Distant Voices, Still Lives* until, finally, *The Long Day Closes*, which is awash with movie references – with Debbie Reynolds singing 'Tammy' thrown in for good measure! And all those films are not without humour, I think.

My work method, with some refinement, has largely remained the same. Over a period of ten to twelve months I make my initial notes. Some sequences come fully formed, others are just mere sketches for scenes – at times containing no more than a scrap of dialogue and a camera movement. Over this period the notes gradually accrete until I have a large batch of material which roughly forms the narrative – although by this time the story has more or less formed itself at the back of my mind. I then sit down and write the first draft from these notes. In this draft every track, pan, dissolve, piece of music and every bit of dialogue appears. Having finished the first draft I leave the text for a while (anywhere between four and six weeks) then sit down and write the second, and final, draft making any necessary changes and adjustments. That is the script we shoot, and the versions of the scripts reprinted here. I *never* do a storyboard. The script is both the storyboard and the shooting script. I go on to the film knowing every shot and camera set-up in the movie as well as what is on the soundtrack at any given point.

Music plays a crucial part in all my films. I was brought up in a house that was filled with music – on the radio, on records and people singing. And, of course, the musical comedy films of the period were part of this. If music is movement and rhythm in time, then film is both movement and rhythm through space *and* time. In *Distant Voices, Still Lives*, the song 'Love is a Many-Splendoured Thing' determined the shots within the cinema sequence, while 'In the Bleak Mid-Winter' was added after the sequence had been written. But music also performs another function in the films. It very often takes over the narrative and becomes the narrative itself when it is not used in counterpoint to the story. For example, in the scene where mum is on the window ledge while Ella Fitzgerald croons 'Taking a Chance on Love', the music and the story become one.

If the music in my films represents my emotional autobiography, the stories represent my actual autobiography, or rather, a version of my life. But with crucial differences. In the Trilogy I was not only exploring literal truth – my relationship with my mother and father, my religious and sexual guilt – I was also examining my terrors; the terror of the death of my mother (whom I adore and who, thank God!, is still with me) and my dread of ending up like the character played by Wilfrid Brambell, dying alone in a geriatric ward.

Distant Voices, Still Lives was much more complicated because it dealt with things I had learned second-hand from my mother and my two eldest sisters and my brother. They talked about my father and the way he had treated them, and their telling of it was so vivid to me that their memories became mine. The difficulty was what to leave out, as their suffering had been so prodigious. But the form of the piece solved my problem. Content dictates form, never the other way round. And as *Distant Voices, Still Lives* was about memory I realized that the form of the films should be cyclical not linear. This decided what could be left in and what had to go. The film constantly turns back on itself, like the ripples in a pool when a stone is thrown into it. The ripples are the memory. But above and beyond this are the enduring constancy of my mother, juxtaposed with the enduring, malign influence of my father. These twin themes permeate the entire film.

The Long Day Closes, on the other hand, is about the loss of childhood paradise and innocence, with the enduring power of the imagination (seen through the movies), and the all-pervasive, all-enduring power of the love of and for my mother. In these films most of the things filmed happened, but not necessarily in that order. I employ a great deal of elision and indeed poetic licence. Whole periods of time are elided into a few seconds of screen time while other moments, insignificant in themselves, are expanded into whole sequences. There is no hard and fast rule. One only has one's instinct and technique to adjust and edit the story one is trying to tell. What I have tried to do in these films is to bring order to the chaos of life – my own and my family's. For there is only chaos below heaven, and each film, book, play, poem or any artistic expression is merely an attempt to impose order on to that chaos. And we never succeed or at least only superficially so. In these films I have attempted to make sense of the mystery of life and also of its magic.

The Trilogy took ten years to complete at a cost of about £46,000. *Distant Voices, Still Lives* took four years to make on a budget of £750,000. *The Long Day Closes* took around three years to make at a cost of £1.75 million. The biggest restriction that these small budgets impose is that of time and the use of expensive machinery. No consideration was given to any budget beforehand; I write the scripts and then make them for the money that it is possible to raise. And I always come in on time and on budget. As the scripts are so detailed it is possible to allocate the money much more effectively. If you know exactly what you are going to shoot, how you are going to shoot and from what camera position, you can cut down wastage considerably. This is also true of the way in which the actors are used. I like to send them the script about a fortnight before shooting and I ask them to read it twice, once for sense and then once more for character. The rehearsal time (just before we shoot the scene) is short – between fifteen and twenty minutes. I like to try to get the shot or scene in less than ten takes (and preferably below five), but obviously with more complicated camera movements the number of takes increases. The Christ sequence in *The Long Day Closes*, for instance, took a large number of takes and nine hours to set up, rehearse then shoot.

But I shouldn't like to give the impression that everything is fixed and that nothing can be changed. That is not so. Everyone on the film can make suggestions and, of course, the actors must be given a certain amount of creative leeway in order to make the roles come alive. I do believe in collaboration, but the film *must* have a central vision and that vision must be the director's.

Once the film is shot the material takes on a new life and, after the first assembly, I never refer to the script again. The images *must* live, the images must *reveal* the story. The intrinsic detail and order changes, but the big sequences always work first time, with a little tweaking. It is at the editing stage that the shot footage reveals its true meaning; this is where the subtext emerges, and the film begins to 'sing'.

It has been a long haul from *Children* to *The Long Day Closes*, but the journey has been immensely rewarding. The only way to learn is to do, and in 'doing' I have learnt to grapple with the complex problems of narrative, rhythm, visual and aural ambiguity – in short all the joy of putting a film together from the initial idea to the final show print.

Whether these scripts or the finished films are liked or not, they were deeply felt and honestly made. All I can say is that I did my best and that the films must stand or fall on their own merits or lack of them. I cannot make an apologia for them, I'm too proud of them for that. The films have many weaknesses but they have strengths too.

In a way they are no longer part of me. They were made with modest budgets and with the most modest of intentions over a very long period of time. Over those eighteen years I think I have achieved an individual style – not to everyone's taste to be sure, but my own. I was lucky enough to find people who believed in my work and was privileged to be able to realize the films in the way I thought best. No director could ask for more.

To all those who have helped, encouraged, produced and worked with me and for me – my profound thanks.

Terence Davies, London, May 1992

TRILOGY

PART I:
Children

The cast and crew of *Children* include:

TUCKER as a boy	Phillip Mawdsley
FATHER	Nick Stringer
MOTHER	Val Lilley
TUCKER at twenty-four	Robin Hooper
BULLY	Colin Hignet
BULLY	Robin Bowen
FIRST TEACHER	Harry Wright
SECOND TEACHER	Philip Joseph
MAN IN SHOWER	Trevor Eve
NEIGHBOUR	Linda Beckett
DOCTOR	Bill Maxwell
NURSE	Elizabeth Estensen
MAN IN BEDROOM	Malcolm Hughes
NEIGHBOUR	Katherine Fahey
NEIGHBOUR	Marjorie Rowlandson

Soloist	Ann Kiesler
Cor Anglais soloist	Stella Dickinson

Lyrics to 'The Ballad of Barbara Allen' from the play *Dark of the Moon* are used by kind permission of the author Howard Richardson.

Written and Directed by	Terence Davies
Executive Production Supervisor	Geoffrey Evans
Production	Peter Shannon
Production Assistant	Rick Thomas
Cameraman	William Diver
Assistant Cameraman	Chris Evans
Assistant Director	Dave Wheeler
Continuity	Anna Maysoon Pachachi
Sound Recordist	Digby Rumsey
Editors	Digby Rumsey
	Sarah Ellis

A British Film Institute Production, 1976

Liverpool in the Late 1950s

Fade up on a high shot of a schoolyard. The main school block is to right of camera and a high wall runs around, from left of camera, to join the building, making a rough triangle. The whole place is an ageing piece of rambling, Edwardian Catholicism.
Cut to a group of five boys consisting of four surrounding a fifth. They stand in the bicycle shed in a semi-circle around TUCKER, *the fifth boy. They are all fifteen.*
Cut to shot of four boys as seen from TUCKER's *point of view. Pan along group.*

BEDSON: Hey . . . who's a fruit then? . . . hey?

CODLING: It's Al Capone, isn't it?

> (*General laughter.*)

MCCABE: Your name's Al Capone, isn't it?

WOODS: Al Capone!

> (*They snigger.*
> *Cut to* TUCKER. *He just stares at them.*
> *Cut back to shot of the four of them. Their fists shoot out in uniform order from left to right, then back again.*
> *Cut to* TUCKER. *He makes no attempt to stop the flurry of blows which catch him in the mouth and chest.*)

TUCKER: (*Thinking*) I won't cry . . . I won't!

> (*Cut to a long shot of the group as they shove and push* TUCKER *around.*
> *Cut to a mouth with a whistle in it. Whistle blows once then after a pause blows again.*
> *Cut back to high shot of yard. All activity stops.*
> *Cut to group. They all exchange frightened looks.*)

BEDSON: (*Whispering*) If you snitch we'll get you tonight.

> (TUCKER *just looks at them.*)

TUCKER'S VOICE: (*Thinking*) I won't cry . . . won't . . .

> (*The whistle blows a third time and they begin to form six lines – each line representing a classroom. The group goes into the first line. Slowly* TUCKER *also goes into this line.*
> *Cut back to high shot. The six lines standing still and the* TEACHER *walking a little distance from them, the whistle still in*

his mouth.)

TEACHER: Right . . . left wheel . . . (*blows whistle.*)
(*The first line turns into the building. He does this for each line.*)

Fade up on a bare classroom on the second floor. There are ten boys scattered about the desks. In one corner BEDSON, CODLING, MCCABE *and* WOODS *all whispering to one another. At a desk by the window is* TUCKER. *All the boys are just in their underpants. At the top of the room two blackboards have been placed together to form a screen, behind which is a doctor.*
Cut to shot of the group whispering and sniggering. Cut to TUCKER.

TUCKER'S VOICE: (*Thinking*) I'm too skinny. I want to get dressed.
(*Cut back to group.*)

BEDSON: (*The words arising out of all the whispering*) . . . Mister Universe . . .
(*Furious sniggering.*
Cut to a shot of room.)

TUCKER: (*Voice over*) Mam . . . I want to get dressed, Mam.

DOCTOR: (*Voice over*) Bedson.
(BEDSON *gets up and goes behind the blackboards.*
Cut to blackboard. Just his legs showing.
A pause.
A cough is heard.
Cut to shot of BEDSON'*s friends exchanging looks and grinning slyly.*
BEDSON *comes out from behind the blackboards and goes to the opposite end of the room where all the clothes are lying in piles. As he passes his friends he grins in a quite revolting way.*
Cut to TUCKER.)

TUCKER: (*Voice over*) Not me! Not me!

DOCTOR: (*Voice over*) Tucker!
(TUCKER *looks across at* CODLING, MCCABE *and* WOODS. *They whisper furiously.*)

CODLING: Mister Universe.
(*Suppressed giggling.*
TUCKER *gets up and goes behind the screen, and the* DOCTOR *starts his examination of him.*)

DOCTOR: Cough.

[4]

(*Cut to* TUCKER's *face. He closes his eyes, then coughs.*
A single giggle is heard.
TUCKER *and* DOCTOR *exchange looks.*)

DOCTOR: (*Smiling*) Well go on . . . you can get dressed now.

TUCKER: Thank you, Doctor.

(*Cut to long shot of room.*
TUCKER *goes to his pile of clothes and gets dressed.*)

DOCTOR'S VOICE: Codling.

(*Cut to the door leading from the classroom.* TUCKER *comes out.*
As he closes the door he looks up and gives a little start.
Cut to BEDSON *lounging at the top of the stairs.*
Absolute silence.
They eye one another. BEDSON *uneasily sadistic,* TUCKER *icily*
contemptuous.
BEDSON *suddenly pushes* TUCKER, *then follows this with a series*
of pushes.
Pause. Silence.
Cut to BEDSON *now unsure what to do.*
Cut to TUCKER *looking at him with a look which drips with*
hate.
A lull.
Quite suddenly BEDSON *lashes out, catching* TUCKER *just below*
the throat. This blow seems to break the spell.
TUCKER *falls on him in a paroxysm of pent up rage and years of*
hate. These blows send BEDSON *reeling down the stairs, but*
TUCKER *doesn't stop raining blow after blow on him. During the*
fight one of TUCKER's *shoes comes off. He picks this up and*
begins hitting BEDSON *with the heel of it.*)

HEADMASTER: (*Voice over*) You two boys – stop that!

(*He comes into shot and separates them.*)

HEADMASTER: Who started this, mm?

(*Silence.*) I suppose you're very proud of yourselves.
(*Silence.*)
I'm very surprised at you, Tucker . . . very surprised. What
have you to say for yourselves?

BEDSON: Nothing, sir.

(TUCKER *still does not say anything.*)

HEADMASTER: Both of you come with me. (*Turns and walks*
away.)

[5]

BEDSON: (*In a whisper*) We'll get you tonight! We'll get you!
   (*They follow the* HEADMASTER.)
   (*Mix to study. The* HEADMASTER *picks up a cane and flexes it.*
   Cut to corridor outside.)
BEDSON: I'm going to get you ton–
HEADMASTER: (*Voice over*) Bedson!
   (BEDSON *halts at the door, rubs his hands, then blows into them*
   and goes in.
   Cut to inside study.)
   Come on–
   (BEDSON *gingerly half-extends his hand. The* HEADMASTER
   makes a strike but BEDSON *pulls his hand away. This is repeated*
   twice. After each miss the HEADMASTER *becomes more niggled.*
   Eventually he grabs BEDSON'S *wrist and brings the cane sharply*
   down twice on BEDSON'S *hand.* BEDSON *squeals.*
   Cut to TUCKER. *The two strokes are heard. After a pause*
   BEDSON *comes out blowing into his hand.*)
BEDSON: Just wait till tonight.
HEADMASTER: (*Voice over*) Tucker!
   (*Cut to* HEADMASTER. TUCKER *enters the study. He extends his*
   hand and receives two strokes, then turns and goes to the door.)
HEADMASTER: Tucker . . .
TUCKER: Yes sir?
HEADMASTER: Aren't you forgetting something?
TUCKER: Sir?
HEADMASTER: (*Shaking his head*) Your shoe, boy . . . put your
   shoe on.
   (TUCKER *realizes that he's still holding his shoe and attempts to*
   put it on.)
   Not here, boy. Outside.
TUCKER: Yes sir.
HEADMASTER: Yes sir.
TUCKER: Thank you sir.
   (*Cut to outside study.* TUCKER *comes out and puts his shoe on,*
   then walks down the corridor.)
   (*Mix to a long rectangular classroom. The* TEACHER *sits at a*
   large table at the head of eight, long, depressing rows of
   desks.
   Cut to long shot of TUCKER *coming in the door.* TUCKER *makes*

[6]

the long journey to his desk at the top of the first row of desks.
Some boys look round at him while the others remain absorbed in
their lesson.)

TEACHER: All right, all right . . . you've seen Tucker before.
(*They resume their work.*
Cut to TUCKER *at his desk. He gets out his exercise book and a*
textbook of English grammar. He rises and attempts to go to the
TEACHER.)

TEACHER: It's 'Subject and Predicate', lad.

TUCKER: Thank you sir. (*Begins to look for the appropriate*
chapter.)

TEACHER: (*Irritated*) Page twenty-five, lad. Page twenty-five.

TUCKER: Thank you sir. (*Sits back down.*)
(*After finding the page he begins the lesson.*
Fade.
Fade up on a wall-clock showing 3.45 p.m.
Cut to high shot of classroom with the TEACHER *walking up and*
down the aisles.
Cut to TUCKER. *He looks up at the clock.*
Cut to BEDSON. *He is deep in his work.*
Cut back to TUCKER.)

BEDSON: (*Voice over*) We'll get you tonight.
(*Cut to clock. It shows 3.50 p.m.*
Cut to TUCKER.
A hand slaps him on the top of the head and he starts.)

TEACHER: I won't forget to tell you when it's time to stop, lad.

TUCKER: Yes sir.

TEACHER: (*Mimicking*) Yes sir.
(*Cut back to high shot of classroom.*
TEACHER *continues his walking up and down the aisles. He*
stops at one desk and looks over a boy's shoulder.)
No, that's not the predicate lad.
(*The boy crosses something out and writes.*)
Neither is that.
(*The boy sits there, at a loss what to do. The* TEACHER *walks*
away, to the top of the class.)
All right, all right, that's it.
(*They stop.*)
Put your things away.

(They do so noisily.)
QUIETLY! Barnes, collect the exercise books.
(A boy gets up and quickly gathers up the exercise books.
Cut to TUCKER. *He looks at the clock. It shows 3.56 p.m.*
Cut to long shot of room.
BARNES *puts the books on the* TEACHER's *desk and resumes his*
seat.)
TEACHER: Right.
(They all stand and join their hands to pray.
As the prayers proceed the TEACHER *continues walking up and*
down the aisles and as they finish he is back at the top of the
classroom.)
ALL: *(Making the sign of the cross)* In the name of the Father and of
the Son and of the Holy Ghost. Amen.

Our Father who art in Heaven Hallowed be thy name, Thy
Kingdom come, Thy will be done on earth as it is in Heaven
. . . Give us this day our daily bread and forgive us our
trespasses as we forgive them that trespass against us . . .
and lead us not into temptation but deliver us from evil.
Amen.

Hail, Mary, full of grace! The Lord is with thee: blessed art
thou amongst women, and blessed is the fruit of thy womb,
Jesus. Holy Mary, Mother of God, pray for us sinners, now
and at the hour of our death. Amen.

Jesus Mary and Joseph I give you my body and blood.
Jesus Mary and Joseph I give you my heart and my soul.
Jesus Mary and Joseph assist me in my last agony.
May I say when I am dying 'Jesus mercy – Mary help'.

In the name of the Father and of the Son and of the Holy
Ghost. Amen.
(They all make the sign of the cross.)
TEACHER: Right, get into line.
(They all step into their respective aisles.)
Turn.
(They do so, so that TUCKER *is now last in the first line and*
BEDSON *is first in his, the third line. The door of the classroom*
now faces the boys.

[8]

Cut to TUCKER. *He looks at* BEDSON.

Cut to BEDSON. *He glances over his shoulder at* TUCKER.)

TEACHER: Eyes front there, boy. Or would you like to lead them out?

(*No reply.*)

Well, go on, lad . . . what would you say?

BEDSON: (*In what he thinks is a posh accent*) Let's go into the schoolyard.

(*Tittering.*)

TEACHER: (*Smiling*) Any more of that and you'll get a kick up the backside . . . or should I say the arse?

(*Roars of laughter from the boys to think that the* TEACHER *would use such a daring word.*)

Goodnight boys.

BOYS: Goodnight sir.

TEACHER: Off you go.

(TUCKER's *line moves off.*)

Quietly.

(*As* TUCKER *draws level with* BEDSON *they exchange looks. Pan with* TUCKER *as he leaves the classroom darting looks over his shoulder.*

Cut to second line moving off. BEDSON *impatient.*

Cut to school entrance. Boys spill out. TUCKER *runs through them and up the street opposite at top speed. Shot of him running to the top of the street.*

Cut back to school entrance. BEDSON *and his three friends come flying out.*)

BEDSON: There he is! There!

(*They begin to run after* TUCKER *at top speed.*

Cut to TUCKER. *Pan with him as he runs frantically along the street.*

Cut back to shot of BEDSON *and* FRIENDS – *head on* – *gasping as they run.*

Cut back to close-up of TUCKER. *He looks back over his shoulder and sees that they are too far behind to catch him. He smiles and begins to pant but runs all the harder.*

Cut to very high shot of TUCKER *being chased by* BEDSON *and Co. They are now mere dots.* TUCKER *turns sharp right, darts across a road and runs down the street where he lives. The*

[9]

pursuers also turn sharp right and cross the road but when they reach the street they stop.
Cut to TUCKER *getting to his front door. Gasping and panting but smiling and safe.*
Cut to group at top of the street. They gasp for breath and glare after TUCKER.
Cut back to TUCKER, *still recovering.*)
TUCKER: (*Voice over*) Safe till Monday.
(*Shot of group walking slowly away as seen from* TUCKER's *point of view.*)

Cut to interior of a doctor's surgery.
Morning. Present day.
Surgery is half empty. Pan camera around room.
Some people read, others stare or look around disinterestedly. Continue pan until camera frames TUCKER's *face. He is now twenty-four.*
The odd cough is heard. Then silence.
A pause.
A buzzer rings and one of the patients gets up and goes through to the doctor's office.
Cut back to close-up of TUCKER. *He sits staring into space. Track in on him.*
Cut to swimming baths. TUCKER – *then fourteen – is seen coming out of a cubicle and into showers which are packed with other boys.*
Cut back to surgery. TUCKER *in big close-up.*
TUCKER'S VOICE: (*Reading a poster*) Say yes to health, say no to smoking.
(*Cut back to swimming-bath showers. Two men come into showers.*
Cut to close-up of TUCKER *at the back of the shower looking at one of the men.*
Cut back to surgery. TUCKER *staring intently straight ahead.*
Shouts of boys in swimming baths are heard echoing.
Cut back to showers. TUCKER *still looking at one of the men. This man has a well-developed physique.*
Cut back to TUCKER *in surgery.*
Cut back to man washing himself.
Cut to TUCKER *at the back of the shower. Boys' voices echoing loudly as they splash about in the water.*

Cut to man. Smiling to himself he finishes washing and then puts his hand down inside the front of his briefs.
Cut to TUCKER *at the back of the shower.*)

A BOY'S VOICE: (*In a whisper*) Look at his muscles!
(*Cut back to* TUCKER *at the back of showers staring in fascinated horror at the man.*
Cut back to TUCKER *in surgery. His eye closing in horror. Shouts echoing. Buzzer goes.* TUCKER *gets up and goes through to doctor's office. Cut to doctor's office.*
TUCKER *comes in and sits down.*)

DOCTOR: (*Without looking up*) Hello, Robbie.

TUCKER: Hello, Doctor.
(*Pause.*)

DOCTOR: And how are we today?

TUCKER: Fine, Doctor.

DOCTOR: Back to work, d'you think?

TUCKER: Oh yes. I'm feeling much better.
And I'd rather be at work anyway.

DOCTOR: And d'you like your work, son?

TUCKER: Yes, Doctor. Very much. It's easy and they're a smashing crowd.

DOCTOR: So you'd like to turn in on Monday.

TUCKER: Please, Doctor.

DOCTOR: Good boy, Robbie.
(*Silence as* DOCTOR *writes out signing-off note.*
Cut to TUCKER. *Zoom in on him.*
Cut to his bedroom. He is standing in front of the wardrobe mirror dressed entirely in leather.)

DOCTOR: (*Voice over*) Mother keeping well, son?
(*Cut back to* TUCKER *staring straight ahead.*)

TUCKER: What?

DOCTOR: Your mother, son. Is she keeping well?

TUCKER: Oh . . . yea . . . you know my mother. Never ails.
Strong as a horse.

DOCTOR: (*Handing him a prescription and note*) Well, stay off for the rest of the week and go in on Monday. I've given you some more tablets for the depression.

TUCKER: Thank you, Doctor.
(*An awkward silence.*)

[11]

DOCTOR: Still no interest in girls yet, Robbie?
>   (TUCKER *shakes his head.*
>   *A Pause.*)
>   Well, that may come, son . . . that may come.
>   (TUCKER *stands up.*)
>   Good-bye. And don't worry, son.
TUCKER: (*Smiling*) Goodbye. And thank you, Doctor.
DOCTOR: Bye, son. Bye, Robbie.
>   (TUCKER *goes out.*
>   *Cut to street. He stands and looks at the traffic droning by.*
>   *Cut to shot of traffic. A bus comes by and there are some children gathered at one of the windows. They look out at* TUCKER. *One of the kids points in* TUCKER'S *direction and says something, and the group laugh.*
>   *Cut to* TUCKER.)
TUCKER: (*Voice over*) They're laughing at me. (*Flatly.*)
>   (*Shot of* TUCKER *walking towards bus stop.*)
>   All dead . . . all dead . . .
>   (*Cut to* TUCKER *at fourteen. Outside his house panting for breath.*)
>   Safe till Monday.
>   (*Cut to shot of group walking slowly away from the top of the street as seen from* TUCKER'S *point of view.*
>   *Cut to* TUCKER *going into house.*
>   *Cut to a curtain – in place of a door – hanging in front of doorway of parlour. Terrible groaning is heard.*
>   TUCKER *stands looking at the curtain. Voices are indistinctly heard. The groans become more and more terrible.*
>   TUCKER *pulls back the curtain.*
>   *Cut to close-up of* TUCKER *staring in horror into the room.*
>   *Cut to shot (over* TUCKER'S *shoulder) of room.*
>   TUCKER'S FATHER – *wearing only longjohns – is rolling on the floor screaming in pain.*
>   *A nurse is trying to get him on to a bed which is pushed up in a corner of this small room. She eventually gets him on to the bed.*
>   *Cut back to close-up of* TUCKER. *Unable to take his eyes off the scene.*
>   *Cut to shot of his father on the bed. He just keeps moaning and*

[12]

*moaning. The nurse stands over him and lifts him so that he is
kneeling on the bed on all fours. She undoes his underwear and
pulls it down revealing father's bare buttocks. She injects him
with morphia.*

Cut to TUCKER *both horrified and fascinated. A squeal is heard
from his* FATHER.)

FATHER: (*Voice over*) You hurt me! You bleedin' hurt me!

(*Cut to* FATHER *struggling into bed. As he settles down he sees*
TUCKER.)

FATHER: How long has he been there? GET OUT!

NURSE: He'll see worse.

(*Cut to long shot –* FATHER's *point of view – of* TUCKER. *He lets
the curtain fall.*

Cut to hall. TUCKER *just stands there, staring at the curtain,
absolutely shocked.*

FATHER's *and* NURSE's *voices are heard arguing.*

MOTHER *comes down the hall carrying two cups of tea.*)

MOTHER: (*Embarrassed*) Hello, son.

(TUCKER *just looks at her then runs upstairs.* MOTHER *looks up
after him, pauses, then goes into the parlour.*

Cut to bedroom. TUCKER *comes running in sobbing and throws
himself on to the bed, face down.*)

TUCKER: (*Through his sobs with the utmost force*) Die you bastard!
DIE!

(*Cut back to bus stop. Bus arrives and* TUCKER *gets on. The bus
moves off.*

Cut to interior of bus. One of the seats upstairs. TUCKER *is
paying his fare. Sitting at the window he looks out.*

Pan with him – from the outside of the bus.

The bus stops at traffic lights.

Zoom in on TUCKER.

Cut to TUCKER *– at fourteen – with his* MOTHER *at bus stop. He
looks at her. They both smile.*

Cut to close-up of MOTHER. *Her face is taut, worried.*

*Fade in introduction to Peggy Lee's record 'The Folks Who Live
on the Hill'.*

The bus arrives. They both get on.)

TUCKER: Can we go upstairs, Mam?

MOTHER: If you like, son.

(*Cut to upstairs. They take their seat,* TUCKER *by the window and* MOTHER *on the outside.* TUCKER *looks out of window and* MOTHER *takes out her handkerchief and blows her nose.*
Cut to outside of bus. Shot of TUCKER *and* MOTHER *looking out of the window.*)
Soundtrack: 'The Folks Who Live on the Hill'.
(*Cut to interior of bus. Silence except for conductor collecting fares.*)

MOTHER: (*To conductor*) Nine and a scholar please.

TUCKER: Look, there's our street, Mam.

(*Cut to outside of bus. Continue panning with bus and* TUCKER's *face.*
Cut to interior of bus.
MOTHER *looks away from the window and at the other passengers. On the verge of tears, her spirit is utterly broken.*)

FATHER: (*Voice over*) There's an 'A' on the ceiling Nellie . . . There's a bleedin' 'A'!

(*She closes her eyes. She begins to cry but tries not to let anyone see her. Her sobs become louder. Her sobs now being noticed by the other passengers,* TUCKER *turns around and looks at her then sinks back into his seat.*)

TUCKER: (*Voice over*) Don't cry, Mam . . . Mam . . . don't cry . . . please . . .

WOMAN PASSENGER: What's the matter, love?

(MOTHER *shakes her head but continues crying.*)

What's the matter, love?

(MOTHER *just shakes her head.*
Cut back to TUCKER *on the bus alone.*
Rain begins to fall against the window.
Cut to exterior of bus disappearing into rain.)

TUCKER: (*Voice over, as a boy*) Mam, I know what that says now . . .

MOTHER: (*Voice over*) Do you, lad?

TUCKER: (*Voice over*) Yes. It says 'Ophthalmic Optician'.

MOTHER: (*Voice over*) You're a good reader, aren't you, lad?

Mix to bus stopping. TUCKER *as an adult gets off and walks into a small block of flats which are nearby.*

Mix to one of the landings in this block. TUCKER *walks into shot. He opens his front door and goes in.*
Mix to interior of flat. The living room.
The front door is heard closing.
TUCKER: (*Voice over*) Mum? Are you in, Mum?
    (*Silence.*
    He enters the living room. Poking the fire he sits down without taking off his overcoat.)

MAN: (*Voice over*) But I like you in leather . . .
TUCKER: (*Voice over*) I feel stupid . . . I just feel soft . . .
    (*Cut to a low-angled shot, side view, of* TUCKER *in his leather gear.*
    A MAN *sits up and coming into shot puts one hand on* TUCKER'S *buttocks and pulls* TUCKER'S *fly down with the other.*
    Cut to close-up of TUCKER.)
MAN: (*Voice over*) Come on baby . . . come on . . .
TUCKER: (*Voice over, exultant, suppressed*) Jesus! . . . oh JESUS!

Cut to TUCKER *in living room.*
TUCKER: God . . . God . . .
    (*From outside laughter is heard. It quickly dies away.*
    Silence.
    Cut to high shot of room. TUCKER *pokes the fire.*)

Cut to close-up of fire being poked. Pause. Then pull camera back to reveal TUCKER'S *father poking the fire.*
TUCKER – *as a boy of fourteen – is sitting with his* MOTHER *on the far side of the small room.*
Silence.
TUCKER – *exhausted – tries desperately to keep from falling asleep.*
Cut to FATHER'S *face.*
Cut to TUCKER, *more and more exhausted.*
Cut to MOTHER.
MOTHER: (*Mouthing to* TUCKER) Don't go to bed . . . don't go to bed . . .
    (*Cut to shot of trio looking at the fire.*
    FATHER *coughs.*)
FATHER: Time for bed . . . You'd better get upstairs . . .

[15]

(TUCKER *and* MOTHER *exchange looks.* TUCKER *gets up and goes out.*

MOTHER *looks after him then lowers her head.*

FATHER *starts poking the fire again.*

Cut to TUCKER *in bedroom. He sits on the bed, listening.*

Silence.

Cut to parlour. Silence.)

FATHER: (*Quietly*) Where is he, eh? Your fancy man . . . where is he? . . . where's Arthur?

(*Pause. His voice becoming louder and louder.*) Did he have it off with you when I was in the army . . .? How many times eh Nell? How many bleedin' times!

After church on Sundays . . .? When I'm out with the cart? Does Peter get some too!

(*In a fury he gets up and, grabbing her hair, pulls her head back.*) Has that bastard been here too? Has he!

(MOTHER – *not retaliating – just cowers.*

Cut to TUCKER *on his bed.*

Slaps are heard.)

FATHER: (*Voice over*) You bleeding cow! You cow!

MOTHER: (*Voice over*) TOMMY! OH TOM!

(*Cut to* FATHER *hitting* MOTHER.

Cut to TUCKER *on his bed.*

Cut to man in showers washing himself.

Cut to FATHER *raining blow after blow on* MOTHER.)

Cut to man's hand going down the front of his briefs.

Cut to TUCKER *on bed. Hands over his ears, his head buried in the pillow, trying not to hear the commotion in the parlour.*

Cut to parlour. MOTHER *on the floor, crying.*

FATHER: (*Sitting looking into the fire*) Shut up! Shut up!

(MOTHER *tries to stifle sobs.*)

Bleedin' shut up Nell.

(MOTHER *gets up from the floor and sits down. She wipes blood off her face.*

Silence.

Cut to TUCKER *lying down on the bed listening intently.*

Vaguely, voices are heard. Then footsteps. MOTHER *comes into*

the room. She goes and sits by TUCKER.
They simply look at one another.
After a pause. She starts to undress TUCKER *and put him to bed.*
When he is finally tucked in she begins to sing him a lullaby.)
TUCKER: Mam . . . oh Mam . . .
MOTHER: 'So close your eyes my little drummer boy . . .
    And say goodnight to all your friends and foes.'

Cut to present day. TUCKER *poking fire.*
He gets up and goes into the kitchen. He makes himself a pot of tea
and some jam and bread. As he does so:
TUCKER: (*Voice over*) How long have you been doing this?
WOMAN: (*Voice over*) The tea and sympathy?
TUCKER: (*Voice over*) Yes.
WOMAN: (*Voice over*) Oh, for years. Since you were a kid.
TUCKER: (*Voice over*) Why?
WOMAN: (*Voice over*) I like to interfere.
TUCKER: (*Voice over*) Oh, stay on the right side, sister.
WOMAN: (*Voice over*) And which side is that?
    (*Pause.*)
TUCKER: (*Voice over*) No one makes bread and jam like you,
    Astyk.
WOMAN: (*Voice over*) Flatterer! It's the trees that are green
    y'know, not me.
    (*Pause.*) What's up, lad? (*Pause.*) Eat your bread, drink your
    tea.
TUCKER: (*Voice over*) You always say that. Remember the first
    time I came in?
WOMAN: (*Voice over*) Yes . . . and you said, 'Oh Astyk I think
    you're a bleeder'.
    (*Both laugh.*)
TUCKER: (*Voice over*) I thought it was a compliment.
    (*Their laughter fades.*
    TUCKER *is now sitting down, sipping tea.*)
TUCKER: Astyk died. Had a heart attack on a dance floor. Oh . . .
    poor Astyk. (*He finishes his snack and goes upstairs.*)

Cut to bedroom. He takes off his overcoat and puts it in the wardrobe-
cum-cupboard. The back of the closet door is completely covered with

[17]

wrestling photos taken during bouts. He runs his hand over them.
Camera pans down these photos. They are of the more violent
American kind.
As the camera pans down the photos, superimpose shouting.
Frame a still of a wrestler's contorted face.
The shouting gets louder.
'Un-freeze' this still and pull camera back.
A wrestling bout in progress. One wrestler in a 'Boston crab'.
Cut to close-up of TUCKER, *at fourteen, sitting in one of the ringside*
seats, wide-eyed at the bout.
Audience roaring.
Cut to close-up of wrestler in Boston crab. His face is almost
unrecognizable as he squeals in pain.
Cut to second wrestler as he applies pressure to the hold.
Cut to TUCKER. *He is almost exultant.*
Crowd roaring, louder and louder.
Cut to close-up of first wrestler's contorted face.
Crowd roaring.
Cut to close-up of second wrestler as he piles the pressure on.
Cut to TUCKER, *almost ecstatic.*
Cut to shot of ring.

FIRST WRESTLER: Yes! Yes!
  (*Roaring.*)
  (*Second wrestler releases hold. General applause.*
  Cut to TUCKER *exhausted. People begin to get up and go.*
  TUCKER *just sits there.*)
ANNOUNCER: And now ladies and gentlemen your appreciation
  for the loser.
  (*Tepid applause.*
  Second wrestler gets down from the ring and is immediately
  surrounded by schoolboys. TUCKER *lurks in the aisle. As the*
  WRESTLER *makes his way past* TUCKER, TUCKER *stealthily*
  touches his thigh.)

Cut back to TUCKER'S *bedroom. He stands staring at the photos. He*
then goes out of the room. Mix to living room. TUCKER *by the fire.*
TUCKER: (*Voice over*) Work on Monday . . . God, what for? . . .
  what do you with time? . . . work on Monday . . . If I say it
  long enough p'raps it'll mean something . . . God . . . God

[18]

. . . there are times – there are times when I desperately want
to feel 'content' . . . 'contentment' . . . like the cow in the field,
like the zombie on the bed . . . work on Monday . . . work . . .
time . . . work and time . . . what have they replaced? I'M
SUFFOCATING TO DEATH! . . . OH GOD! I need
something to believe in again . . . work on Monday . . . oh God
. . . oh Mam . . . Mam . . . Mummy . . .

CHILDREN'S VOICES: I believe in God the Father, Almighty,
Creator of Heaven and earth, and in Jesus Christ, His only
son, Our Lord.
(*Cut to children spilling out of primary school gates. Fade voices.*)
TUCKER: (*Voice over, superimposed*) I was happy then Mummy . . .
I was happy . . .
(*Mix to a school back yard. Children – all about eleven – march
four abreast towards the camera. They are wearing fancy dress.
Cut to a high shot of school yard. Children marking time in front of
a window.
Cut to window.
A semi-circle of parents around the window. They applaud.
Under the window a small school choir. Through the open window
a teacher plays the piano.
Cut back to high shot of school yard.
The choir begins to sing but their singing is indistinguishable.
Zoom slowly in on the choir.
As the camera gets nearer to it the singing becomes audible.
Everything else is still.*)
TUCKER: (*Voice over*) Way down upon the Swannee River . . .
CHOIR: (*Singing*) 'Way down upon the Swannee River,
Far far away, There's where my heart is yearning ever,
There's where the old folk stay.
All up and down the old plantation,
Sadly I roam,
Oh darkies how my heart grows weary,
Far from the old folks at home.'
(*Cut back to* TUCKER *in living room.*)
TUCKER: (*In tears*) Miss Delaney! Miss Delaney!
(*A single note of a piano is heard being struck.*)
WOMAN: (*Voice over*) (*Singing note*) Mmmmm . . .

[19]

CHILDREN: (*Voice over*) (*Singing note*) Mmmmm . . .
    (*This is repeated twice.*)
WOMAN: (*Voice over*) The old folks at home.
CHILDREN: (*Voice over*) (*Singing*) 'Way down upon the Swannee
      River,
      Far far away,
      There's where my heart is yearning ever,
      There's where the old folks stay.'
    (*Fade voices.*)
TUCKER: (*Voice over*) And 'Whistling Rufus The One Man Band'.
    (*Silence.*)
    Negro Spirituals . . . Miss Delaney liked negro spirituals . . .
    and Stephen Foster . . .
    (*Almost reverie.*)
    Jeffrey Whitby's eyelashes . . . Swing low – sweet Cha-r-i-ot . . .
    (*Cut back to* TUCKER.)
TUCKER: Bang! Bang! You're dead.

Cut to high shot of small parlour room. FATHER *is on the bed and the
room is filled with people standing around it.*
FATHER: (*His voice barely audible*) I can see angels at the foot of
    the bed, Nell . . .
    (*A* PRIEST *leans over him murmuring extreme unction.*
    GRANDMOTHER *looks at* MOTHER *and shakes her head.*
    MOTHER's *face crumbles into tears.*
    Cut to TUCKER. *He is transfixed by the body of his father on the
    bed.*)
A VOICE: Death . . . death.
    (*Cut to high shot of the room directly over the bed.*
    The priest finishes the last sacraments and straightens up.
    The room is very still, very bright, very hot.)
PRIEST: God rest his soul.
GRAN: He's gone . . . My Tommy's gone . . .
    (MOTHER *is convulsed in sobs.*
    *Zoom slowly in on the corpse of the father and his long, rigid
    features.*
    Cut back to TUCKER.)
A VOICE: He's stiff!

(*Cut back to high shot of the bed.*
Continue slow zoom in on father.
Cut to TUCKER.)

A VOICE: That smell . . . it's him that's smelling.
(*Cut back to high shot of bed.*
Continue zoom, until father's face is framed. GRAN *places*
pennies on father's eyes.
Cut to side view of father's head.
Cut to TUCKER. *His jaws are being forced together seemingly by*
their own volition. He holds his head and begins to rock to and
fro faster and faster. A sound like that of an animal is heard
coming through his clenched teeth.)

TUCKER: NNNNNNNNNN! NNNNNNNNNN!
(*He rushes from the parlour.*
Cut to doorstep. TUCKER *comes flying out and sinks down on the*
doorstep.
Pause.)

TUCKER: The bastard's dead . . . we're free, Mam . . .

Zoom in on his hunched figure on the doorstep. When he is framed in
close up, hold, then freeze, then blur vision.
Clear vision. TUCKER *is still sitting on doorstep but now he holds a*
loaf. It is two days later, early evening.

TUCKER: (*Voice over*) I'm frightened to go in . . . past the parlour
. . . I'm scared . . .
(*Cut to high shot of parlour.*
FATHER *lies in coffin. The rest of the room is filled with flowers*
from floor to ceiling.
Cut back to TUCKER *on doorstep.*
Pull camera back to reveal two women peering down at him.)

FIRST WOMAN: Is your mam in, lad?

TUCKER: Yes, Mrs May.

SECOND WOMAN: Can you tell her – we've come to see your dad.
(TUCKER *just sits there.*)

FIRST WOMAN: Go on lad. Go on.

TUCKER: I'm scared, Mrs May. I'm scared.
(*She puts her arm around him.*)

FIRST WOMAN: What of, lad?

[21]

TUCKER: I'm too scared to go past the parlour.

SECOND WOMAN: Well, your Dad can't hurt you now, son.

FIRST WOMAN: The dead can't bite.

TUCKER: (*In a paroxysm*) I'm scared, Mrs May!
I'M SCARED!

FIRST WOMAN: Well you run in and tell your mam we're here . . .
We'll watch you.

> (TUCKER *stands up, waits for a minute, then rushes in.*
> *The two women look after him. The* FIRST WOMAN *shakes her*
> *head and tuts.*)

Mix to high shot of parlour. The two women stand looking into the
coffin.
Silence.

FIRST WOMAN: Well he won't feel any more pain now, Nellie . . .
God help him.

> (MOTHER *nods. Silence.*)

SECOND WOMAN: I liked Tommy. He always let on when you
passed.

> (*Pause. Then the women start looking at the wreaths and reading*
> *the condolence cards attached to them.*)

MOTHER: (*After a long silence*) Thanks for the wreath . . . it was
lovely.

FIRST WOMAN: We wanted to.

> (*Pause.*)

SECOND WOMAN: It was the least we could do.

> (*A long silence as the three of them stare into the coffin.*)

FIRST WOMAN: Well, Nellie, we'd better be going.

MOTHER: Thanks for coming.

SECOND WOMAN: T'ra Nell.

> (*All three leave the room.*
> *Superimpose* FIRST WOMAN's *voice as camera lingers in high*
> *shot of room.*)

FIRST WOMAN'S VOICE: I liked Tommy . . . I knew him well.

Mix to mother's bedroom in total darkness. It's about 2 a.m. the
following morning. It is a large, sparse room. It contains a double bed
in which the mother is asleep.
Cut to TUCKER's *bedroom. A single bed in which* TUCKER *lies.*

[22]

Cut to TUCKER. *He is awake.*
He lies perfectly still listening hard.
Slowly he comes into a sitting position.
Silence.
He listens hard.
A long pause.
Silence.
He gets up and waits.
Absolute silence.
*Slowly he leaves the bedroom on tiptoe, goes to the head of the stairs
and looks down.*
TUCKER: (*In a hushed whisper*) Mam!
    (*Nothing.*)
    (*Hushed whisper*) Mam!
    (*Nothing.*
    Cut to bottom of stairs. TUCKER's *face is framed at the top of
    them. To the right of camera, light is seen under the kitchen door.*
    Cut to inside the kitchen.
    Several people sit drinking tea in absolute silence.
    Cut back to the bottom of the stairs.
    TUCKER *gingerly makes his way down them. He slowly goes to
    the kitchen door and listens.*
    Silence.
    *Very slowly he makes his way along the hall to the parlour and
    stands in front of the curtain.*
    *For a while he stands there unable to pluck up enough courage to
    lift the curtain.*
    Slowly he pulls the curtain up. He steps inside.
    *Mix to shot of parlour now lit only by candles. Mid-high shot
    from sideboard end.*
    TUCKER *comes and stands at right of frame.*
    Stillness.
    Mix to close-up of TUCKER *rivetted by the coffin.*
    Mix to coffin.
    Mix to flowers.
    Mix to shot of parlour.
    Cut to TUCKER *through candles' flame walking towards the
    coffin.*
    Cut to coffin. TUCKER *walking towards it.*

[23]

Cut to flowers.

Cut to TUCKER *walking towards coffin as seen from coffin's point of view.*

Cut to coffin with FATHER's *face showing.* TUCKER *left of scene.* TUCKER, *now terrified, rushes from the room.*

Cut to the hall. TUCKER *running upstairs.*

Cut to bedroom. TUCKER *comes flying in and throws himself on the bed. Blur vision.*

Clear vision: bedroom the next morning. TUCKER *sits on the bed dressed in his funeral clothes.*

Pause.

He lifts his arms to his face and sniffs the material. He then lifts the corner of his jacket and sniffs that. He goes to the window.

Mix to shot of the street as seen from TUCKER's *point of view. Neighbours throng around the front door and the four funeral cars. The undertakers' men are loading the wreaths on to the hearse.*

Mix to the parlour. They are screwing the coffin lid down.

Mix to the bedroom. TUCKER *looks at the floor. Superimposed the squealing of cats. A child's voice is heard:* 'Don't kill them . . . don't kill the kittens.' *Shot of* FATHER *kneeling on the bedroom floor dropping kittens into a bucket of water. They squeal, they struggle: they drown, then float around in the water dead.*

Cut back to TUCKER. *He hides his face in the curtains.*

Mix to shot of hall. The mourners – all in black – leave the kitchen. The group is headed by TUCKER *and* MOTHER.

Zoom or track back from this group as they come down the hall. The coffin is loaded into the hearse. At the head of the group of mourners, TUCKER *comes out. He stops and looks down into the street.*

Cut to street and cortège as seen from TUCKER's *point of view. All eyes seem to be on him.*

Pan camera around their faces full circle and finish with close-up of TUCKER's *profile.*

A slight pause. TUCKER *quite suddenly bursts out into a single laugh.*

Mix to long shot of cortège. All get into the cars and the cortège moves off.

*Mix to graveside. A man with a shovel full of dirt offers it to each
mourner.* MOTHER *first, then* TUCKER *and so on. They throw
their handfuls of soil into the grave. Mix to* MOTHER's *face.)*

MOTHER: (*Voice over*) Oh love . . . oh love.

(Silence.

Mix to TUCKER's *face.*

*Cut to him lying in his bedroom, his hands over his ears trying to
blot out* MOTHER's *screams of* 'Oh Tommy . . . Tom . . .'

Cut to wrestling ring. A wrestler's contorted face.

Cut to man in showers.

Cut to TUCKER; *present day, in living room, closing his eyes.*

Cut to other man pulling his fly down.

Cut to graveside.)

TUCKER: (*Voice over*) Bastards! Bastards!

(Silence. All look into the grave. MOTHER *still crying.*

Cut back to living room. TUCKER *present day.)*

TUCKER: Dad . . . Dad . . . please say that you love me, Dad . . .

(Cut back to graveside. They stand looking into the grave.

Mix to parlour.

Cut back to graveside.

They stand looking into grave.)

Mix to parlour. They have returned from the cemetery. MOTHER *sits
there in an armchair – frozen, expressionless.* TUCKER *looks at her.
Then he goes to her and begins to stroke her hair. She just sits there and
stares ahead.*

*Silence. As he continues to gently stroke her hair, she takes his other
hand in hers.*

Mix to kitchen. TUCKER *stands by the window looking out.*

Mix to outside shot of TUCKER *looking through window.*

Mix back to Tucker inside. Silence.

Mix back to outside shot of TUCKER *looking through window. Hold.
Then begin to zoom very slowly away and fade in 'The Ballad of
Barbara Allen' being sung by the unaccompanied voice of a girl.*

BALLAD: 'A witch-boy from the mountain came,

A-pining to be human,

For he had seen the fairest girl . . .

A girl named Barbara Allen.'

Mix back to TUCKER *in kitchen.*

[25]

Silence.

TUCKER: (*Near to tears*) Oh Dad . . . Dad!

(*Mix back outside to shot of* TUCKER. *Continue to zoom away.*)

BALLAD: 'O Conjur Man, O conjur man,
    Please do this thing I'm wanting,
    Please change me to a human man,
    For Barbara I'd be courting.'

(*Mix back inside to* TUCKER.

This time the ballad is heard inside kitchen. TUCKER *is crying.*)

BALLAD: 'Oh you can be a man, a man,
    If Barbara will not grieve you,
    If she be faithful for a year,
    Your eagle he will leave you.'

(*Mix back to outside shot of* TUCKER.

*Continue zooming slowly away until his face and the window
and the house become smaller and smaller.*)

BALLAD: 'O Barbara will you marry me
    And will you leave me never
    Oh yes my love I'll marry you
    And live with you for ever.'

TRILOGY

PART 2:
Madonna and Child

The cast and crew of *Madonna and Child* are as follows:

TUCKER (middle-aged)	Terry O'Sullivan
MOTHER	Sheila Raynor
TATTOOIST	Paul Barber
PRIEST	John Meynall
MAN IN CLUB	Brian Ward
TATTOOED MAN	Dave Cooper
SECOND MAN	Mark Walton
MAN IN TOILET	Mal Jefferson
WOMAN IN OFFICE	Lovette Edwards
WOMAN IN OFFICE	Rita Thatchery
MAN IN OFFICE	Eddie Ross
Written and Directed by	Terence Davies
Production	Mike Maloney
Cameraman	William Diver
Assistant Cameraman	Sergio Leon
Assistant Director	Kees Ryninks
Continuity	Victoria McBain
Sound Recordist	Antoinette de Bromhead
Grip	Tim Rolt
Editor	Mick Audsley
Dubbing Editor	Geoff Hogg

A National Film School Production, 1980

Liverpool: The Present

Fade up on

EXT. PIER HEAD. LIVERPOOL. DAY

*It is early morning, and cold. Close-up of a seagull wheeling in the sky
above the River Mersey.*
Pan with it, following its flight.
Dissolve to other angles of the bird in close-up and medium close-up.
Over this, a children's choir singing – echoing and distant – :
CHOIR: 'Hail Queen of Heaven, the ocean star,
      Guide of the wanderer here below,
   Thrown on lifes' search we claim thy care,
      Save us from peril and from woe.
   Virgin most pure, Star of the sea,
   Pray for the wanderer, pray for me.'
*Then a series of pans and dissolves as camera follows other birds in
flight, wheeling in the sky and dipping over the river.*
Dissolve to high shot of the river, looking out towards the sea.
Pan to the Birkenhead ferry at berth or about to dock.
Cut to:

INT. BUS COMPLEX. PIER HEAD

TUCKER *in medium close-up coming down through the first bus tunnel
going towards the pier head. He is in sharp focus but the background/
surround is blurred.*
Cut to mid-shot of TUCKER *walking down second bus tunnel on his
way to pier gangway.*
Cut to bottom of pier gangway. TUCKER *walks down.*
Cut to:

EXT. LANDING STAGE. PIER HEAD

TUCKER *comes towards the Wallasey ferry berth and waits.*
Cut to TUCKER'S *point of view of Birkenhead ferry. The boat moves
away from the landing stage. We watch it drift to mid-river. The
Wallasey ferry is also mid-river getting closer quickly, about to dock.*
Cut to TUCKER *in medium close-up. He looks cold and tired. He*

*yawns. Then his face settles back into impassivity. He seems near to
tears.*
Cut to Wallasey ferry docking and passengers disembarking.
A ferryman goes by.
Cut to side-view of TUCKER *in close-up. He follows the ferryman as
he walks across and looks out to sea.*
*Cut to shot of the ferryman. He takes a drag on his cigarette then flicks
it into the river. His arm is noticeably tattooed.*
Cut to:

INT. BEDROOM. NIGHT
*Close-up of a man. He is naked to the waist. He smiles then turns his
head to the right and looks down. The camera slowly travels from his
face down over his heavily tattooed chest and arm until it frames his
hand. Camera stops.*
The man lifts his forefinger and TUCKER's *head comes into frame. He
is smiling. He looks up. He licks the man's forefinger then, taking the
entire finger into his mouth, he sucks it.*
Cut to:

INT. FERRY. DAY
TUCKER *gets up from the seat and goes to the gangway in order to
disembark.*
Cut to TUCKER *in medium close-up. Liverpool receding further and
further away in the background.*
Cut to close-up of TUCKER (*Back view*) *waiting to disembark.
Wallasey pier getting closer and closer.*
Cut to:

EXT. WALLASEY LANDING-STAGE
The gangplank comes crashing down. TUCKER *disembarks.*
Cut to long shot from top of gangway. TUCKER *walks up. He gets to
the pay booth and pays.*
Cut to:

EXT. WALLASEY FERRY BUILDING BUS DEPOT
TUCKER *comes out of the entrance. Pan with him.*
Cut to TUCKER *walking down by the side of the bus depot building.
A single stroke on a kettledrum is heard.*

Cut to:

INT. BACK OFFICE. LATER THAT MORNING
Side view of TUCKER *in close-up. He is absorbed in his work.*
Silence except for someone's continual coughing and wheezing.
Distant phones ringing. Office sounds – dull and far away. Track
around desks in medium shot. At the first desk – a man thirty-six,
balding. He is working. Continue track. At the second desk – a
woman twenty-six. As she works she sucks a sweet. Continue track. At
the third desk – a woman, late fifties. She is coughing/wheezing
continually. Stop track when she is framed. She takes a drag on her
cigarette then stubs it out.
WOMAN: (*Without looking up and in between coughs*) Did you go
    anywhere at the weekend?
Cut to:

INT. TUCKER'S BEDROOM. NIGHT
Low angle shot of TUCKER's *feet going into cowboy boots.*
Cut to TUCKER's *thighs. He is squeezing into very tight jeans, cut to*
TUCKER *putting on a polo-necked sweater then a leather bomber*
jacket. All this business is done in the dark and very carefully so that
no one will hear.
Cut to:

INT. MOTHER'S BEDROOM. NIGHT
Shot of MOTHER *in bed, asleep.*
Cut to:

INT. LANDING CONNECTING THE TWO BEDROOMS. NIGHT
Low angle shot of TUCKER's *feet coming through his bedroom door.*
Pan with him to the head of the stairs. He treads very carefully so that
he will make no noise.
Cut to:

INT. BOTTOM OF THE STAIRS. NIGHT
TUCKER *stands at the top of the stairs perfectly still. Silence. He steps*
forward. A creak is heard.
Cut to TUCKER *at the top of the stairs in close-up. He freezes and*
listens. Silence. Long pause. He leans towards mother's bedroom door.

[31]

TUCKER: (*In a hoarse whisper*) Mam . . . Mam . . .
Cut to:

INT. MOTHER'S BEDROOM. NIGHT
MOTHER *moves in her sleep, sighs, then blinks half-awake but she is
still very drowsy.*
Cut to:

INT. LANDING. NIGHT
TUCKER *in close-up. Dead silence. Pause.*
Cut to low angle shot of TUCKER's *feet. He treads very gingerly on to the
first stair.*
Cut to:

INT. MOTHER'S BEDROOM. NIGHT
MOTHER *stirs and murmurs something in her sleep. Still very sleepy she
gradually blinks awake and listens.*
Cut to:

INT. HALL. NIGHT
TUCKER – *seen from the bottom of the stairs – he descends very slowly
and quietly.*
Cut to:

INT. MOTHER'S BEDROOM. NIGHT
MOTHER *leans up on one elbow – listening intently.*
Cut to:

INT. HALL. NIGHT
TUCKER *reaches the hallway and goes quietly to the front door. Pan
with him. He begins – very slowly and gingerly – to take off the alarm
bell chain.*
Cut to TUCKER *in close-up. He bends down and begins to draw the bolt
back from the bottom of the front door. It squeaks loudly. He stops and
listens. Dead silence.*
Cut to:

INT. MOTHER'S BEDROOM. NIGHT
MOTHER *in close-up. She is straining every nerve listening. Dead silence.*

[32]

Cut to:

INT. HALL. NIGHT

TUCKER *at the front door. He slides the bolt back. Then quietly opens the front door and goes out.*
Cut to:

EXT. FLAT'S LANDING. NIGHT

TUCKER *comes out of the flat. He closes the front door very quietly and with equal care comes through the gate, making sure that he leaves it open.*
Cut to:

INT. MOTHER'S BEDROOM. NIGHT

MOTHER *in bed. Pause. Then she eases herself back against the pillows. She is wide awake. Her eyes wide – she is near to tears.*
Cut to:

EXT. FLAT'S LANDING. NIGHT

Shot of TUCKER. *He smirks to himself, then walks down the landing feeling his crutch.*
Cut to:

INT. BACK OFFICE. DAY

WOMAN: (*Repeating the question*) Did you?
(*Cut to* TUCKER *in close-up. He looks surprised. Pause.*)
TUCKER: (*Nervous, hesitatingly*) . . . No . . .
(*He continues working but is obviously very disturbed. Hold this shot for a long time.*
Dissolve to tracking shot around desks. Feet in medium close-up. At the first desk – the man's feet. His left foot on the ground his right foot on its tip. Continue track. At the second desk – the woman's feet. Her legs crossed. Continue track. At the third desk – the woman's feet. Her legs crossed behind her. Dissolve to close-up of woman's mouth at third desk. She is coughing through her clenched fist. Track around desks. Close-up of woman at second desk. She is sucking a sweet. Continue track. Close-up of man at first desk. He is sucking his teeth. Continue track until TUCKER *is framed in close-up. Track stops. Silence.* TUCKER

[33]

looks at them in utter disbelief.
Cut to:)

EXT. STREET. DAY

Shot of the black stones of a wall. Track slowly left to right. A man is
seen standing in a doorway. He is looking down the street to his left.
He takes a drag on his cigarette. He is very heavily tattooed on the
chest and arms. Continue track until shop window is framed. Stop
track. The window is covered with designs for tattoos and reads:
'JACKS – TATTOO ARTIST' *(and telephone number).*
Cut to:

EXT. STREET. DAY

TUCKER *in close-up. Track with him as he walks past tattoo shop. He*
looks extremely tense.
Cut to:

INT. CHURCH. EVENING

Three tracking shots over which there are continuous voice overs.
Track one: the camera tracks from left to right along the side aisle over
the first six Stations of the Cross. Over this, dialling/ringing/and pips
heard. Money being put into a phone box. Pause.

MAN: *(Voice over) (Short, sharp)* Jacks!

TUCKER: *(Voice over) (Extremely nervous)* Is that the tattooists?

MAN: *(Voice over)* Yer . . .
   (A long pause.)

TUCKER: *(Voice over) (Almost choked with nerves)* I . . . er . . . I
   want my bollocks tattooed . . .

MAN: *(Voice over) (Decisively)* I won't touch a prick for less than
   twenty notes . . .
   (Pause.)

TUCKER: *(Voice over) (Desperate)* Will you do it?
   (Slight pause.)

MAN: *(Voice over) (Bending very slightly)* It takes a helluva fuckin'
   time . . . I've got a tattoo on me own chopper and it took me
   three days to get it on . . . besides it hurts like fuck . . .

TUCKER: *(Voice over) (Very desperate)* Will you do it?

MAN: *(Voice over) (Bending a little further)* Apart from the time it
   takes, its gotta be as hard as a biscuit . . . you'll be wankin'

[34]

off by the minute . . .
(*A very long pause.*)

TUCKER: (*Voice over*) (*Almost to himself*) Please say you'll do it.
Please!
(*A complete silence.*)

MAN: (*Voice over*) (*Matter-of-fact*) . . . what d'you want on it
anyway?

TUCKER: (*Voice over*) (*Reviving a little, a ray of hope but still very
nervous*) I want 'fuck' down the back of my cock in big black
letters and a swastika on each of my balls . . .
(*Silence.*)
(*Pleading.*) Will you do it?
(*Silence.*
*Dissolve to track two: the camera tracks from right to left along
the back aisle looking down towards the high altar.*)

MAN: (*Voice over*) (*Uncertainly*) Well . . . I mean . . . you might
have a dose. I do it for you then three weeks later I'm
scratchin' the bollocks off meself . . .
(*Dissolve to track three: the camera tracks from left to right over
the last six Stations of the Cross.*)

TUCKER: (*Voice over*) (*Quickly*) You won't get a dose off me.

MAN: (*Voice over*) (*Snapping back*) Yer – that's what they all say
when they come in here – and a lotta guys want their bollocks
tattooed . . .

TUCKER: (*Voice over*) (*Trying to resolve the situation*) Will you do it
for me?

MAN: (*Voice over*) (*Still annoyed*) It's no skin off my fuckin' nose
. . . but it'll cost yer . . . if I hold a prick in me hand I want
payin' – thirty notes – no messin'!
(TUCKER *does not answer. An anguished silence.*)

TUCKER: (*Voice over*) (*Trance-like*) When can I come round?

MAN: (*Voice over*) (*Perfunctory*) No – I won't touch a prick for less
than fifty.
(*And the line goes dead.*
End of track.)

Cut to:

INT. CHURCH. EVENING
Side view of MOTHER's *hands in close-up clasped – praying. She*

[35]

holds rosary beads.
Cut to Side view of MOTHER *and* TUCKER *in two shots kneeling in confessional pews.* MOTHER *crosses herself and moves to sit back in pew.*
Cut to Medium close-up of MOTHER *and* TUCKER *in two shots.*
MOTHER *sitting in pew.* TUCKER *still kneeling. He is praying, although his prayer is inaudible. Pietà in background. He finishes praying and moves back and sits in pew beside* MOTHER.
Cut to close shot of them both sitting in pew. Pietà in background. Silence.
Cut to side view of MOTHER *and* TUCKER *sitting outside confessional box. A penitent comes out and* TUCKER *gets up and enters confessional box.*
Cut to:

INT. CONFESSIONAL BOX

Blackness. Silence. Pause. TUCKER *is seen kneeling down at the grille. He is just discernible in the darkness. He makes the sign of the cross.*
TUCKER: (*As he does so*) In the name of the Father, and of the Son, and of the Holy Ghost. Amen.
  (*The priest momentarily lifts the curtain behind the grille then drops it back again.*)
  Bless me Father, for I have sinned.
PRIEST'S VOICE: (*Barely audible*) May the Lord be in your heart and on your lips, that you may, with truth and humility, confess all your sins, in the name of the Father, and of the Son, and of the Holy Ghost. Amen.
TUCKER: I confess to Almighty God, to Blessed Mary, ever Virgin, to Blessed Michael the Archangel, to Blessed John the Baptist, to the holy apostles Peter and Paul, and to all the saints, that I have sinned exceedingly, in thought, word, and deed, through my fault, through my fault, through my most grievous fault. Pray, father, give me your blessing. It is three weeks since my last confession and I accuse myself of missing Mass on Sundays through my own fault – three times, taking God's holy name in vain – many times, being disobedient – four times, being proud – twice . . .
  (TUCKER's *voice begins to fade. Pan away from him, from left to right, to blackness.*)

Coveting my neighbour's goods – three times . . .
(*His voice now completely gone. Pan ends. Blackness.*)
Oh, you've got a fucking gorgeous arse!
(*Cut to:*)

INT. BEDROOM. NIGHT

Pan from right to left, to medium close-up of TUCKER. *He sits on a bed.*
On the extreme left of frame a man stands – back to camera – facing TUCKER. *The man is visible only from the waist to the knees. He begins to unbuckle his belt and jeans.*
When he has unbuckled the belt and undone the top of his jeans he stops. A pause. TUCKER *then pulls the man's jeans slowly down and he is naked underneath them. A pause.* TUCKER *looks up at the man then directly at the man's crotch.* TUCKER *then opens his mouth very wide. As camera tracks from right to left behind the man so that his buttocks entirely fill the frame. Slight pause. Then* TUCKER's *hands come into shot being placed on the man's buttocks.* TUCKER's *hands clutch at man's buttocks once – then twice.*
Cut to:

INT. CONFESSIONAL BOX

Blackness. Pan right to left until TUCKER *is framed. He is still kneeling at the grille.*
TUCKER: (*Fade up his voice*) . . . dishonouring my parents – many
    times, despairing – many times, borne hatred – three times.
    (*Long pause.*)
    That is all I can remember, father.
    (*The* PRIEST *raises the curtain.*)
PRIEST: (*From behind the grille*) Is there anything else you wish to
    confess, my son?
    (*Cut to close-up of* TUCKER *seen from the* PRIEST's *point of view
    through the grille.*)
TUCKER: (*Wanting desperately to speak but unable to do so. Shakes
    his head*) No father . . .
    (*Curtain is dropped.*
    Cut to shot of TUCKER *kneeling at grille.*)
    (*With no conviction, almost despair*) For these and all other
    sins that have escaped my memory, I am heartily sorry,

[37]

humbly ask pardon from God, and penance and absolution from you Father.

(*The words of absolution are spoken by the* PRIEST.)

PRIEST: (*Voice over, ending*) . . . and for your penance say three Hail Mary's, two Our Fathers and one Glory Be. God bless you, my son.

TUCKER: Thank you Father.

(*He just kneels there in the darkness.*
Cut to:)

EXT. ALLEY. NIGHT

TUCKER – *in medium long shot – is seen coming down an alley and stopping at a door. He knocks.*

Cut to TUCKER *in close-up at the door. It has a grille in it. Getting no reply he knocks again. A small door behind the grille slips back.*

YOUNG MAN: (*From behind the grille throughout*) Yer?

TUCKER: (*Trying to sound very masculine*) Are you open yet pal?

YOUNG MAN: (*Suspiciously*) This is a gay club.

TUCKER: Yes, I know.

YOUNG MAN: I haven't seen you here before.

TUCKER: I came here about two years ago.

YOUNG MAN: Who with?

TUCKER: A mate.

YOUNG MAN: (*Not convinced*) Oh.

(*He snaps the grille-door shut.*
Cut to:)

INT. CHURCH. EVENING

Close up of crucifix on the high altar.

Cut to TUCKER *kneeling at altar rails saying his penance. His prayers peter out and he looks at the cross. Pause. He closes his eyes in horror, covering his face with his hands.*

TUCKER: Say but the word, and my soul shall be healed.

(*A single stroke on a kettledrum is heard.*
Cut to:)

INT. BACK OFFICE. DAY

General shot of the four desks. Silence. Then a siren is heard and everyone gets up and exits. It is lunchtime.

[38]

Cut to:

INT. CANTEEN. DAY

Long shot of TUCKER *at centre canteen table eating his sandwiches and surrounded by his colleagues at other tables. He is seen across the billiard table at which three men are playing. Very slowly track and zoom in on* TUCKER.

INTERCOM: Call for Mr Maxwell . . . telephone call for Mr Maxwell . . .
    (*Continue track and zoom.*)

FIRST MAN: (*As second man sinks a ball*) Wonderful fucking shot!

SECOND MAN: Oh fuck!

THIRD MAN: Fucking great stuff!

MAN: (*At one of the tables behind* TUCKER) I got some conti-board and woodstained it . . . then I varnished the hardboard . . . I'm bloody made-up with them shelves . . .
    (*Track and zoom stops. Side view of* TUCKER *in close-up. He has stopped eating his sandwiches.*)

INTERCOM: (*Annoyed*) Calling Mr Maxwell! . . . telephone call for Mr Maxwell!
    (TUCKER *turns and looks at the men who are playing billiards, right at camera. It is a look which drips with a mixture of loathing, anger and longing. His eyes fill with tears. Cut to:*)

EXT. STREET. NIGHT

Low angle shot of TUCKER'S *feet. He is wearing cowboy boots and walking along pavement. Track with him.*
Cut to:

INT. TOILETS. NIGHT

Silence except for dripping water. Semi-darkness. Low-angled shot of TUCKER'S *feet coming into toilets. Track with him as he goes to one of the urinals and stands there. Hold. Then track slowly along to next but one urinal and frame a man's feet.*
Cut to close-up of TUCKER. *He is looking down. Pause. He then looks right towards man. Cut to close-up of man at other urinal. He is also looking down.* TUCKER *coughs, and the man looks left towards him. Pause. Then the man passes his tongue nervously across his lips.*

Cut to long shot of TUCKER *and man standing perfectly still at their respective urinals, their backs to camera. Silence. A long pause. Then* TUCKER *moves to urinal next to man. A long pause. Then simultaneously their hands reach towards one another.*
Cut to:

INT. FILING AND RECORDS OFFICE. DAY

Immediately after lunch. Rows and rows of files are stacked. TUCKER *comes swiftly in and bangs the doors shut as if in an absolute fury and walks to the files. He gets a file down and begins to go through it. Track slowly in on him. As we get closer he stops reading and stares at the papers, then looks up. He begins to cry.* TUCKER *now in close-up. He is sobbing. His crying reaches a climax then begins to subside. Track back from him to mid shot. He stops crying. He wipes his eyes and blows his nose.*
Cut to:

INT. BOARDROOM. DAY

Late afternoon. Long shot of TUCKER *from the end of the board table. He looks towards us.*
Cut to long shot of man from TUCKER's *point of view at other end of table speaking into the telephone, although what he is saying can only be faintly heard.*
Cut to side or back view of TUCKER *in close-up. He is looking towards us. Pause. He sighs, then looks out of the window.*
Cut to:

INT. DAY

TUCKER *is seen coming slowly down the corridor outside the boardroom. Pan with him as he turns into reception. He goes upstairs.*
Cut to:

INT. GENERAL OFFICE. LATE AFTERNOON

Mid shot of TUCKER *coming through the door. He is seen through the glass panelled inner office. Pan with him.* TUCKER *goes to a desk in the outer office and begins to go through the day book.*
Man at desk in inner office looks around then taps on the glass partition and beckons TUCKER *in.*
Cut to:

INT. BACK OFFICE. LATE AFTERNOON
Pan around office. All the desks are empty and cleared. Frame
TUCKER *in close-up. He is still at his desk. He bangs a filing cabinet*
shut and then tidies his desk. He finishes tidying up then rubs his face
with his hands. Then he stares straight ahead. It is a look of
weariness, mingled with despair.
Cut to:

EXT. STREET. LATE AFTERNOON
Shot of TUCKER *as he walks over the first iron bridge in Birkenhead.*
VOICE OVERS: Good night June . . .
>   Good night Lynn . . .
>   Nigh-night Chris . . .
>   Night . . .

Cut to TUCKER *walking down a street in Birkenhead with Victorian*
lamp-standards along it.
Cut to TUCKER *walking across second iron bridge in Birkenhead.*
Cut to:

INT./EXT. FERRY BUILDING/BUS DEPOT. WALLASEY.
LATE AFTERNOON
TUCKER *walks down the gangway towards ferry berth.*
Cut to mid shot of TUCKER *from behind looking towards Liverpool*
waiting for the ferry to dock. From the same angle ferry docks and
TUCKER *boards.*
Cut to mid-shot of TUCKER *from behind at gangway on ferry looking*
towards Liverpool, waiting for ferry to dock. Ferry docks. TUCKER
disembarks.
Cut to:

EXT. STREET. LATE AFTERNOON
Bus stops and TUCKER *gets off and walks across waste ground*
towards flats. Pan with him.
Cut to long shots of blocks of flats.
MOTHER: (*Voice over*) I've done a bit of sausage and mash for your
>   tea . . . with some onion gravy . . . OK, lad?
TUCKER: (*Voice over*) Yes, Mam . . .
Cut to:

INT. TUCKER'S FLAT. BATHROOM. NIGHT
It is full of steam. TUCKER *stands in the bathroom and brings his hands to his face and luxuriously wipes his face and neck and chest. Cut to:*

INT. LIVING-ROOM. NIGHT
Medium shot of TUCKER *on settee. TV is on.* TUCKER *is watching it. He looks across at his* MOTHER. *Pan to* MOTHER. *She sits on the other side of the settee, her mouth open.*
Cut to close-up of TUCKER. *He is still looking at* MOTHER.
Cut to close-up of MOTHER, *her hands lying in her apron.*
Cut to close-up of TUCKER.

TUCKER: (*Very softly*) Oh, Mam . . .
    (*Cut to* MOTHER. *Her head droops. Her mouth is open. She stirs in her sleep.*)
MOTHER: (*Half-awake, half-asleep*) Oh, I'm dead licked . . .
    (*Dissolve to shot of living-room from behind the settee. TV is off.* TUCKER *is looking straight ahead.* MOTHER *is asleep. Silence. Dissolve to shot of* MOTHER *winding clock.*)
MOTHER: See you in the morning lad . . .
    (*Pan with her to the door.*)
    I'll lock up . . .
    (*Cut to side view of* TUCKER *in close-up from behind the settee.*)
TUCKER: OK Mam. D'you want some cocoa later on?
    (*Cut to* MOTHER *at door.*)
MOTHER: Yer . . . goodnight son . . .
    (*She exits.*
    Cut to side view of TUCKER *in mid close-up.*)
TUCKER: Good night Mam. God bless.
    (*Cut to front view of* TUCKER *in close-up. He listens to the door being bolted then the sound of his* MOTHER *climbing the stairs. Dissolve to:*)

INT. LIVING-ROOM. NIGHT
Shot of TUCKER *pulling the hearthrug back several inches from the grate.*
Cut to shot of TUCKER *fluffing then rearranging the cushions on the settee.*
Cut to shot of TUCKER *switching off the lights in the living-room.*

Cut to shot of TUCKER *pouring hot milk into his mother's cup.*
Dissolve to:

INT. MOTHER'S BEDROOM. NIGHT

Shot of TUCKER *coming into her bedroom carrying a cup of cocoa.*
The room is lit only by the landing light. TUCKER *sits on the bed.*
TUCKER: (*Softly*) Mam . . .
    (*Gently shakes his* MOTHER.) Mam . . .
    (MOTHER *wakes up.*)
    Here's your cocoa, Mam.
    (*He gives her the cup of cocoa. Taking the cup she sits up in bed.*)
MOTHER: (*Sipping her cocoa*) Thanks lad . . . You're a good
    boy . . .
    (*She continues sipping her cocoa.* TUCKER *continues sitting on*
    the bed. They just look at one another.
    Dissolve to close-up of MOTHER *lying in bed asleep. Her mouth*
    is open.)

INT. TUCKER'S BEDROOM. NIGHT

Side view of TUCKER *in close-up. He is in bed, asleep. His face is*
turned away from the camera. He sighs and stirs in his sleep.
VOICE OVER: (*Long, low and sibilant*) P – A – R – I – O –
    L – E – Y!
    (TUCKER *turns. His face is now in profile.*)
VOICE OVER: But know thou that for all these things God will
    bring thee into judgement. For God shall bring every work
    into judgement, with every secret thing, whether it be good
    or whether it be evil.
    (*Cut to:*)

EXT. FLAT'S LANDING. DAY

It is overcast. Grey. Slightly unreal. Four men carry a coffin down the
landing. They are seen head on.
TUCKER's *head immediately above and behind the coffin. He looks*
terror-stricken. The cortège moves towards the camera.
VOICE OVER: And further, by these, my son be admonished . . .
    put away evil from thy flesh . . .
    (*Cut to:*)

[43]

EXT. FLAT'S ENTRANCE. DAY

A very high shot of the coffin from the top of the flats looking directly down. The coffin comes into shot. It appears to float into frame as the four men carry it.

VOICE OVER: For the souls of the righteous are in the hands of
  God . . .
  (*Cut to:*)

EXT. FLAT'S ENTRANCE. DAY

Head on shot of coffin carried by four men, with TUCKER's *face and head immediately above and behind coffin.* TUCKER *looks terror stricken.*

VOICE OVER: And there shall be no torment to touch them . . .
  (*Cut to:*)

INT. CHURCH. DAY

Low-angle shot of the feet of the four men carrying the coffin very low. Track with them down centre aisle. They place the coffin on trestles.

VOICE OVER: And the fruits that thy soul lusted after are
  departed from thee . . . The time is at hand . . . Thy
  judgement is come.
  (*Cut to low-angled shot from inside the coffin. The faces of the
  four men look down at the camera. They are all impassive.*)

VOICE OVER: The judgement and the mercy of God.
  (*A single stroke on the kettledrum is heard.*
  Cut to high shot of coffin in centre aisle. TUCKER *is in it. His eyes
  are open. Begin a very slow zoom in on to his terror-stricken face.
  He tries desperately to speak but cannot. His mouth twitches as he
  tries to open it.*)

TUCKER: (*Trying desperately to speak*) . . . A . . . a . . . shs . . . st
  . . . sti . . . sti . . . sti . . . gu . . . cru . . . ddd . . . drup . . . cru
  . . . c . . . ccc . . . cour . . . age . . . Cruda . . . cru . . .
  cruuuuuu . . . A . . . ha . . . haha . . . ha . . . ha . . . daas . . .
  das . . . de, de, de, de, . . . De-eeeee . . . De-eeeee . . .
  nnnnnnn . . . nnnnnnoooooo!! . . . nnnnooooo . . .
  pppppppooooorr, or . . . Poor . . . poor-ra-ta . . .
  ahmmmmnoodahafirstistimmoommnna . . . na . . . ma . . .
  ma . . .
  (TUCKER *in extreme close-up.*)

[44]

Mm! . . . Mm! . . .
(*Cut to:*)

INT. TUCKER'S BEDROOM. NIGHT

TUCKER *is seen head on in close-up sitting up violently.*

TUCKER: MM . . . MM . . . MA! . . . HHHAAAHAAA!!

    (*He is sobbing uncontrollably. Hold.*
    Cut to shot of MOTHER *in bedroom doorway. She is a black silhouette in an 'Our Lady' stance.*)

MOTHER: Are you all right, lad?

    (*Cut to* TUCKER *head on in close-up.*)

TUCKER: (*His sobs subsiding but a look of terror still on his face*) Yes . . . Mam . . .

    (*He calms down a little as he realizes where he is. He lies back down.*
    Cut to shot of MOTHER *closing bedroom door.*
    Cut to side view of TUCKER *in close-up. He lies down, his head touching the pillow. He lies in profile looking at the ceiling. Pause. Then he turns his face towards the camera.*)
    (*Tears in his eyes*) Yes . . .
    (*He begins to sob – stifled and despairing. He continues to cry softly. Begin a very very slow fade to black. He continues crying. His face disappears altogether. Blackness. His crying is faintly heard. It finally subsides altogether.*
    Blackness.
    Absolute and complete silence. Then:)

TUCKER'S VOICE: (*Howling like an animal in peril*) M – A – M!!!

    (*Silence. Pause. Fade to black.*)

TRILOGY:

PART 3
Death and Transfiguration

The cast and crew of *Death and Transfiguration* are as follows:

TUCKER as an old man	Wilfrid Brambell
TUCKER middle-aged	Terry O'Sullivan
TUCKER at eleven	Iain Munro
MOTHER	Jeanne Doree
NURSE	Chrissy Roberts
NURSE	Virginia Donovan
NUN	Carol Christmas
WARD SISTER	Angela Rooks
DOCTOR	Brian Gilbert
NURSE	Katharine Schofield
NEIGHBOURS	Ron Metcalfe
	Lisa Parker
	James Wilde
	Ron Jones
	James Culshaw
	Marie Smith
	Jim Penman
	Gerry Shaw
	Mandy Walsh
BOY AT WINDOW	Paul Oakley

Children from The McKee School

Written and Directed by	Terence Davies
Executive Producer	Maureen McCue
Production	Claire Barwell
Make-up Advisor	Fae Hammond
Art Director	Miki van Zwanenberg
Cameraman	William Diver
Continuity	Helena Barrett
	Carine Adler
Sound Recordists	Mohammed Hassini
	Charles Patey
	Mark Frith
Editor	William Diver

A Greater London Arts production with the BFI (1983)

Fade up on:

EXT. LIVERPOOL. DAY
A shot looking out to sea with clusters of corporation flats in the foreground. It is very early.
Cut to:

EXT. STREET. DAY
Close shot of car doors being banged shut.
Soundtrack over the whole of the following of Doris Day singing: 'It All Depends On You'.
Cut to:

EXT. STREET. DAY
Close-up of radiator grill.
Cut to:

EXT. STREET. DAY
Medium long shot of people looking towards camera.
Cut to:

EXT. STREET. DAY
Low angled side view shot of wheels of limousine. They glide slowly away, left to right, followed by one other car.
Cut to:

EXT. STREET. DAY
Close shot of headlamps flashing as the first car turns left to right.
Cut to:

INT. PASSENGER CAR. DAY
Passenger's point of view of leading car – which is a hearse. It carries a coffin and wreaths.
Cut to:

INT. PASSENGER CAR. DAY
Side view of passenger. It is TUCKER, *aged about fifty-five years. He*

[49]

is in silhouette. The streets glide past.
Cut to:

INT. PASSENGER CAR. DAY

Close-up of TUCKER'*s hands.*
Cut to:

EXT. STREET. DAY

Medium long shot of hearse, head on, coming towards camera.
Cut to:

INT. HEARSE. DAY

Close-up side view of driver and second man.
Cut to:

EXT. STREET. DAY

Medium close-up of coffin and wreaths seen through the glass of the
hearse. The hearse glides past from left to right.
Cut to:

Shot of birds flying from the trees. Darkness is gathering.
Cut to:

A shot of the sun large and low in the sky.
Cut to:

EXT. CEMETERY GATES. DAY

Mid-shot of cars gliding in through the gates of Yewtree cemetery.
Cut to:

EXT. CEMETERY. DAY

High long shot of cars driving up the long gravel drive of the cemetery,
seen from the gates.
Cut to:

Close shot of the cars coming to a halt.
Men get out of hearse.
Cut to:
Men carrying coffin shoulder high followed by a single mourner. It is

TUCKER.
Song ends.
Cut to:

INT. CREMATORIUM. DAY
End of coffin close-up gliding into the oven on rollers. The curtains and doors at the far end close. Pause. Then suddenly the oven flames burst upon the coffin.
Title:

Death and Transfiguration

Cut to:

INT. GERIATRIC WARD. VERY EARLY MORNING
TUCKER *is seen in medium long shot from the foot of his bed. He is much older now – in his late sixties.*
Two nurses at either side of his bed have just finished washing him and rubbing his pressure areas. They finish.
FIRST NURSE: There you go, Pop . . . spick and span.
SECOND NURSE: Spruce.
(*As they draw towards the end of his bed brushing the bedclothes down, back in on* TUCKER. *He seems very ancient as he lies motionless in bed.*)
FIRST NURSE: (*Voice over*) What's pink, wrinkled and hangs out your underpants?
SECOND NURSE: (*Voice over*) I don't know.
(*Track stops. Old* TUCKER *in big close-up.*)
FIRST NURSE: (*Voice over*) Your mother!
(*Both nurses giggle.* TUCKER *just looks at them, then his eyes flicker forward and he stares straight ahead. His mouth begins to move as he tries to form a word.*
Cut to:)

INT. CAR. DAY
Side view of TUCKER *in close-up (aged fifty-five), returning from funeral. He tries to say mother but cannot.*
PRIEST: (*Voice over*) I am the resurrection and the life.
(*Cut to:*)

[51]

EXT. CORPORATION FLATS. DAY

The funeral cars drive into shot. Tucker gets out.

PRIEST: (*Voice over*) See, O Lord, and consider

How is the gold become dim,

How is the most fine gold changed.

(*Cut to:*)

INT. FLAT. DAY

TUCKER *in medium-long shot sitting at the kitchen table. A cup of tea beside him. Silence. Then slowly he begins to sip his tea. Pause. Cut to:*

INT. TUCKER'S BEDROOM. DAY

TUCKER *sits on his bed with a scrap-book on his lap. He turns the pages.*

Cut to TUCKER'S *point of view of scrap-book. It is filled with photographs of wrestlers and naked, muscular young men which he has cut out of magazines and pasted in. He stops at one page and passes his hand over a certain photograph. Then he leans down and kisses it. Cut to:*

INT. MOTHER'S BEDROOM. DAY

Medium shot of MOTHER'S *wardrobe. The door is open. Her clothes hang neatly from the rail. Her shoes are on a neat row below them. Cut to:*

INT. MOTHER'S WARDROBE. DAY

Close-up of garments hanging from the rail. TUCKER'S *hands enter shot and touch her clothes. Cut to:*

INT. MOTHER'S BEDROOM. DAY

Side view of TUCKER *in close-up at wardrobe. He just stands there looking at her clothes. His eyes fill with tears as he buries his face in one of her coats.*

TUCKER: Mam . . . Mum . . . Mummy . . .

(*Cut to:*)

INT. GERIATRIC WARD. EARLY MORNING

Head on close-up of old TUCKER. FIRST NURSE *finishes feeding him his breakfast.* SECOND NURSE *pumps up his pillow.* TUCKER *eases back. One of the* NURSES *walks towards a window at the end of the ward. Pan with her left to right until hospital window is framed. Outside it is pouring with rain.*

FIRST NURSE: (*Voice over*) Christ, what a day!
    (*Pause.*)
SECOND NURSE: (*Voice over*) Roll on Christmas.
    (*Cut to:*)

EXT. STREET. DAY

Shot of grey morning sky. It is pouring with rain. Pan down right to left from sky, past house fronts to TUCKER *from a three-quarter side view as a boy of seven or eight. He is hurrying to school. Track with him. He begins to hurry a little faster.*
Soundtrack:

CHILDREN: (*Voice over. Praying*) 'Jesus, Mary and Joseph,
    I give you my heart and my soul . . .'
    (*He breaks into a trot.*
    Soundtrack:)
    'Jesus, Mary and Joseph, I give you my body and blood . . .'
    (*He begins to run. Track stops. Pan with him as he runs past camera.*
    Cut to:)

INT. JUNIOR SCHOOL. DAY

TUCKER *in close-up. Track back with him as he runs down corridor towards his classroom.*
Soundtrack:

CHILDREN: (*Voice over. Praying*) 'Jesus, Mary and Joseph, Assist
    me in my last agony . . .'
    (*Cut to* TUCKER's *point of view of classroom door at the end of the corridor. Track in on it.*
    Soundtrack:)
    'May I say when I am dying
    Jesus – mercy, Mary – help.'
    (*Track stops.* TUCKER *walks into shot and listens at the classroom door.*

[53]

Soundtrack:)
'In the name of the Father, and of the Son, and of the Holy Ghost, Amen.'
(*Sounds of the children sitting down. Then, quite suddenly, a cough is heard and* TUCKER *looks quickly back over his shoulder. From* TUCKER'S *point of view in medium long shot cut to the headmistress standing at the other end of the corridor. She is a nun and is in silhouette, her hands clasped in front of her.*)

HEADMISTRESS: (*Very softly*) There's no need to run inside the school, Robert.
(*Cut to side view of* TUCKER *in close-up from classroom door.*)

TUCKER: No, Sister.
(*Pause. He waits for a moment, then gingerly knocks on the classroom door. He enters.*
Cut to:)

INT. JUNIOR SCHOOL CLASSROOM. DAY

TUCKER *comes in and walks towards camera. To his left a coal fire blazes.*

TUCKER: I'm sorry I'm late, Miss Walsh.

MISS WALSH: (*Voice over. Kindly*) Stand by the fire until you're dry then go and see Sister.

TUCKER: Yes Miss.
(*He wipes his face with his hand, then gets out his handkerchief and begins to wipe his hair with it.*
Cut to:)

INT. MAIN CORRIDOR JUNIOR SCHOOL. DAY

Long shot. The main corridor is empty. Pause. Then footsteps are heard. TUCKER *enters frame right from around the corner. He is dressed as an angel. He walks towards camera. His steps slow to a stop. He stands there for a moment. Pause. Then he bursts into a fit of giggles. They eventually subside. Silence. He walks to the door of the* HEADMISTRESS'S *study and knocks softly.*

HEADMISTRESS: (*Voice over. Softly*) Come in.
(*He goes in and closes the door.*
Cut to:)

INT. HEADMISTRESS'S STUDY. DAY

Side view of TUCKER *in close-up.*

TUCKER: Good morning Sister.

   (*Cut to:*)

INT. GERIATRIC WARD. DAY

Medium close-up of ward sister. She is switching off the lights.

WARD SISTER: Good morning boys!

   (*Cut to first man in geriatric ward. He is seen from a three-quarter side view in medium long shot, sitting in a chair across from his bed. He stares straight ahead.*

   Soundtrack:)

HEADMISTRESS: (*Voice over*) Who made you?

CHILDREN: (*Voice over*) God made me.

   (*His hand goes up to the side of his head and scratches it. He then lays his hand down on the bed in front of him.*

   Cut to second man in geriatric ward. He is seen from a three-quarter side view in medium long shot. He is being helped on to a commode at the side of his bed by two nurses.

   Soundtrack:)

HEADMISTRESS: (*Voice over*) Why did God make you?

   (*Cut to third man in geriatric ward. He is seen from a three-quarter side view in medium long shot. He eats porridge very slowly from a plate. When he has finished he lets the spoon fall into the plate.*

   Soundtrack:)

CHILDREN: (*Voice over*) God made me to know Him, love Him and serve Him in this world and to be happy with Him for ever in the next.

   (*Cut to side view of* TUCKER *in big close up in bed (à la Man Ray's photograph of the ageing Sibelius).* TUCKER *stares straight ahead.*

   Soundtrack:)

HEADMISTRESS: (*Voice over*) What is God?

CHILDREN: (*Voice over*) God is love.

   (*Cut to:*)

INT. CHURCH CONFESSIONAL. DAY

TUCKER *as a boy enters and closes confessional door. In the darkness,*

[55]

TUCKER's *form can just be made out as he stands there. Pause. He then begins feeling around the walls for the grille. Eventually he thinks he has found it and kneels down directly in front of the camera.*

TUCKER: Pray Father, give me your blessing, this is my first confession and I accuse myself of . . .

(*Over* TUCKER's *right shoulder we see a curtain drawn back.*)

PRIEST: (*From behind the grille*) I'm over here.

(*Cut to:*)

INT. GERIATRIC HOSPITAL CORRIDOR. DAY

Long shot of old TUCKER *being wheeled up corridor in a wheelchair, towards camera, by a* NURSE. *As they get to a series of windows on their left which overlook an inner courtyard, the nurse stops and puts the brakes on the wheelchair.*

NURSE: (*To* TUCKER – *rather too loudly*) I'm just going for your X-rays, Mr Tucker . . . So I'll leave you here for just a minute . . . OK?

(*He doesn't respond. She walks away. Hold.*

Cut to close-up of old TUCKER *from the front. He looks old and sick. The right side of his mouth is slightly twisted. Hold.*

Soundtrack:)

DOCTOR: (*Voice over. Echoing slightly as if he were explaining to a group of medical students*) Cerebral thrombosis – stroke – stroke syndrome: a condition with sudden onset caused by acute vascular lesions of the brain . . .

(TUCKER *turns and looks out of the window and down on to the inner courtyard. Pan slowly with him.*)

(*Soundtrack:*)

. . . such as haemorrhage, embolism, or rupturing aneurism . . .

(*Pan stops when window is framed. Outside it is raining heavily. Soundtrack:*)

. . . which may be marked by hemiplegia or hemiparesis, vertigo, numbness, aphasia and dysarthria . . .

(*Hold camera on window. Pause.*

Soundtrack:)

It is often followed by permanent neurological damage and or death.

(*Hold camera. Pause. Then pan back to:*)

[56]

INT. HOSPITAL CORRIDOR. DAY

Pan stops when TUCKER *at fifty-five is framed in close up. He is looking out of the window at the rain.*
Soundtrack:
MOTHER: (*Voice over*) You mustn't grieve, lad . . .
(*Doors are heard banging open.* TUCKER *looks around, full face to camera.*
Cut to – from behind TUCKER *– a medium long shot of ward doors opening. Visitors move towards them.* TUCKER *follows them, carrying an umbrella.*
Soundtrack:)
MOTHER: (*Voice over*) When I die . . . say you won't grieve . . .
(*Cut to:*)

INT. HOSPITAL WARD. DAY

Close-up of MOTHER *in bed. She lies in bed, semi-conscious, tubes up her nose and down her mouth. She has no teeth. She half-wakes, turns her head towards* TUCKER *– slowly – then smiles very weakly at him.*
Cut to TUCKER *in close-up at the bedside. He tries to smile but is too close to tears.*
TUCKER: (*With great difficulty*) How are you Mam? . . . How do you feel?
(*Cut to* MOTHER *in close up. Her smile fades. Her eyes close again.*
Two shot side view of TUCKER, *left of bed.* TUCKER *gently takes* MOTHER's *hand, rubs it then gently cradles it in his hand.*)
TUCKER: (*Very softly, through tears*) Mam, oh Mam . . .
(*Cut to:*)

INT. GERIATRIC HOSPITAL CORRIDOR. DAY

Side view of old TUCKER *in close-up sitting in wheelchair. Except for hospital noises, silence as he looks out of the window. Pause. Then the hospital noises begin to fade and we hear laughter echoing.* TUCKER *slowly turns his head and looks up. The laughter continues.*
Cut to:

INT. LIVING-ROOM. NIGHT

High two shot of MOTHER *in her eighties and* TUCKER *at fifty-five seen over* MOTHER's *shoulder. They are both laughing.* MOTHER *sits on the couch,* TUCKER *sits on a stool in front of her, cradling her foot in his lap.*

TUCKER: (*Through giggles*) Oh Mam, don't laugh . . . otherwise we'll never get it done . . .

> (*Cut to medium long shot of* MOTHER *and* TUCKER *in side view from* TUCKER's *position.*)

MOTHER: (*Through giggles*) Oh! . . . you're a bloody case! . . .

> (*The laughter subsides. He begins to bandage her lower ankle.*)

TUCKER: How has it been today, Mam?

> (*Cut to close-up of* MOTHER.)

MOTHER: It was aching a bit this morning . . . not much though . . .

> (*Cut to close-up of* TUCKER.)

TUCKER: You shouldn't stand on it, you know . . . you're supposed to rest with a leg ulcer . . .

> (*Cut to close-up of* MOTHER.)

MOTHER: I do rest it . . . honest, lad . . .

> (*Cut to close-up of* TUCKER.)

TUCKER: (*Finishes bandaging*) Oh, you'd say that . . .

> (*Medium long shot of* MOTHER *and* TUCKER *in side view from* TUCKER's *position.*)

MOTHER: Read our stars . . . Go on lad.

> (TUCKER *picks up the paper and finds the right page.*)

TUCKER: (*Reading*) Capricorn . . . (*Reads stars.*)

MOTHER: And what's yours?

TUCKER: (*Reading*) Scorpio . . . (*Reads stars.*)

> (*It is something improbable.*)

Oh chance'd be a fine thing.

MOTHER: Well, you never know your luck in a big city.

> (*They both smile.*)

TUCKER: Fancy a cuppa?

MOTHER: Aye . . . I wouldn't say no.

> (*He gets up to go out of the room. He gets to behind the sofa, immediately behind his* MOTHER.
> *Cut to high two shot over* TUCKER's *shoulder looking down on to* MOTHER. *She looks up at him as he bends over her. He takes her face in his hands.*)

TUCKER: (*Looking down at her*) Oh – what would I do without you?

> (*Cut to:*)

INT. AGAINST BLACK DRAPES

Close-up of a head being pulled into shot. (NB: this is not TUCKER.*)*
The head is entirely encased in a leather head mask which has open
zips over the eye and mouth holes. A dog collar is around this first
man's neck. A dog lead is attached to the collar by a large d-ring.
Soundtrack:
SECOND MAN: (*Voice over*) Use your teeth . . .
    (*Cut to:*)

INT. BOOKSHOP. DAY

Close-up of TUCKER *at fifty-five seen through the window from inside*
the bookshop. As he looks into the shop his head is framed like a halo
surrounding it by S+M and soft gay porn magazines which are
hanging up.
A customer, third man, enters frame. He is wearing tight leather jeans.
His buttocks entirely fill the frame.
Soundtrack:
SECOND MAN: (*Voice over*) Pull the zip down . . .
    (*Cut to:*)

INT. AGAINST BLACK DRAPES

Medium long shot.
SECOND MAN *stands with his legs wide apart. He is stripped to the*
waist and very muscular. He is wearing tight leather jeans, boots,
wriststraps, sunglasses and a motorcycle cap.
In front of him kneels first man (head and shoulders only). He is
wearing the head mask and collar and is stripped to the waist also. He
faces SECOND MAN.
SECOND MAN *pulls first man to him.*
SECOND MAN: Use your fucking teeth!
    (*Cut to:*)

INT. BOOKSHOP. DAY

Close-up of third man's buttocks from inside shop.
Soundtrack:
SECOND MAN: (*Voice over, half in pain, half in ecstasy*)
    Nnnaaarrrhhh!
    (*Third man's buttocks clear frame.*
    TUCKER *revealed in close-up still looking through window. He*

stands there a moment looking very tense.
Then lowers his eyes.
Cut to:)

INT. CHURCH. DAY

Side view of TUCKER *in close-up as a boy kneeling at the altar rails with his mouth wide open.*
Soundtrack:
CHILDREN: (*Voice over, singing*) 'Jesus thou art coming,
  Holy as thou art . . .'
 (TUCKER, *with his mouth still open, is waiting to receive Holy Communion. He holds the paton under his chin.*
 Soundtrack:)
 'By the God who made me,
  To my sinful heart . . .'
 (*The* PRIEST's *hands come into shot. They hold a chalice. The* PRIEST *takes a host from the chalice and puts it into* TUCKER's *mouth.*
 Soundtrack:)
 'Jesus I believe it,
  On thy only word . . .'
 (TUCKER, *having received the Eucharist, bows his head.*
 Cut to:)

INT. GERIATRIC WARD. NOON

Mid shot of ward sister sitting at her desk at the far end of the ward.
Soundtrack:
CHILDREN: (*Voice over, singing*) 'So shall I never, never part from thee.'
 (*Singing fades.*
 Two nurses come in, past desk, carrying a large natural Christmas tree into the ward.)
FIRST NURSE: Hello, Staff.
STAFF NURSE: Hello, girls . . . wouldn't this weather put years on you?
SECOND NURSE: They say it'll snow for Christmas.
FIRST NURSE: Oh, she's cheerful isn't she?
 (*All smile. The two nurses exit frame.*
 Cut to close-up of a cup of tea on bedside locker. A pair of hands

[60]

*slowly enter frame and shakily pick up the cup. Pan right to left
with cup until three-quarter side view of old* TUCKER *is framed in
close-up. He is sweating profusely and looks weak. He sips his
tea.*
Cut to long shot of two NURSES *putting Christmas tree at the
other end of the ward. Through the window it is raining.*
Cut to front view of old TUCKER *in close-up being lifted into an
upright position by two nurses. As he is being lifted, he looks very
weak. Clearly everything is becoming an extreme effort.)*

FIRST NURSE: Now then . . . there we go . . .
    (*Cut to:*)

INT. CHILDREN'S HOSPITAL. DAY

Medium close-up in side view of TUCKER, *as a boy, being lifted into
an upright position by a* DOCTOR.

DOCTOR: Now then Robert . . . take a really deep breath in . . .
    (TUCKER *does so.*)
    . . . Hold it . . .
    (TUCKER *does so.*)
    And now . . . let it slowly out . . .
    (TUCKER *does so.*
    Cut to MOTHER *aged thirty-five with* TUCKER *as a boy walking
    down corridor away from camera.* TUCKER *looks up at her.*
    Soundtrack:*)
DOCTOR: (*Voice over*) Good boy, Robert . . .
    (*Cut to:*)

INT. GERIATRIC WARD. AFTERNOON

Three-quarter side view medium long shot of old TUCKER *being helped
to the side of his bed by two* NURSES. *With every movement* TUCKER
keeps saying, very weakly, over and over again:

TUCKER: Oh . . . Oh . . .
    (*When they have got him to the side of his bed, they hold a bottle
    for him to urinate into.
    Soundtrack:*)
TUCKER: (*Voice over, as a boy*) Why do I have to have breathing
    exercises, Mam?
MOTHER: (*Voice over*) It'll help your cough, lad.
    (*Cut to:*)

[61]

INT. SHOPPING PRECINCT. DAY

MOTHER *aged eighty,* TUCKER *aged fifty-five, in medium long shot three-quarter side view walking down one of the aisles towards camera. They walk slowly.* TUCKER *carries the shopping.*
The shops are decorated and advertising for Christmas.

MOTHER: We've been invited to Elaine's twenty-first.

TUCKER: On Saturday?

MOTHER: Yer . . . Christmas Eve.

TUCKER: Oh, smashin'.

    (*Soundtrack: voices singing 'Abie, Abie, Abie My Boy'.*
    Cut to:)

EXT. STREET. NIGHT

Medium-long shot of TUCKER *as a boy standing on the corner of the street outside a pub. Snow is on the ground.*
Soundtrack: they sing 'Abie, Abie, Abie My Boy'.
TUCKER *rises on tiptoe trying to see into the pub through the frosted glass.*
Soundtrack of the song continues.
Sound mix to next song.
Cut to long shot of group of adults coming down the street from pub, towards camera. They are in silhouette, and singing as they walk.
Soundtrack of people in the pub singing 'How You Gonna Keep Them Down on the Farm'.
Cut to TUCKER *as a boy in medium close-up sitting on the doorstep. The adults rapidly walk past him into the house, singing.*
Cut to high shot of adults coming into the parlour as seen through the window from the street.
Through the window the parlour can be seen to have been decorated for Christmas. At the window a small natural Christmas tree. Everyone is dancing and singing.
Cut to close-up of a pair of woman's hands and arms, outstretched. It is MOTHER *but we don't see her face.*
Soundtrack: RENEE'S *voice over, trying to sing above the general hubbub of the parlour 'There's a Someone to Watch Over Me'.*
MAN: (*Voice over, shouting*) Order! Go on Renee. Order *please!*

    (TUCKER *as a boy walks into shot and the outstretched arms and hands wrap around him.*
    Soundtrack: RENEE *singing.*

TUCKER *hugs his* MOTHER *to him and smiles up at her.*)
MOTHER: (*Voice over*) Happy Christmas lad.
TUCKER: Happy Christmas Mam.

(*And slowly, in a small circle, they begin to dance to* RENEE'*s
singing.*
Cut to high shot of MOTHER *and* TUCKER *slowly turning as they
dance. It begins to snow.*
Soundtrack: RENEE *finishes her song.*
The people in the parlour applaud. MOTHER *and* TUCKER *keep
dancing – silently in the falling snow.*
Soundtrack: people singing 'If You Knew Suzie'.
Cut to:)

INT. FLATS. NIGHT

Sound mix.
Soundtrack: continues song. Begin to fade singing. Singing gone.
MOTHER *aged eighty*, TUCKER *aged fifty-five get out of lift and
walk along landing away from camera.*
TUCKER: (*Voice over*) It was a good night, wasn't it Mam?
MOTHER: (*Voice over*) Yer . . . smashin'.

(*Cut to:*)

INT. HOSPITAL. DAY

Close-up of two X-ray photographs illuminated. They are of
TUCKER'*s skull. One from the side, one from the front. Hold.*
Soundtrack:
PRIEST: (*Voice over*) 'And the Angel of the Lord said unto
them . . .'

(*Cut to:*)

INT. GERIATRIC WARD. LATE AFTERNOON

Track slowly up TUCKER'*s bed from foot of bed.*
Soundtrack:
PRIEST: (*Voice over*) '. . . Fear not, for I bring you tidings of
great joy which shall be to all the world . . .'

(*Track stops. Side view of* TUCKER *in close-up. He is sweating
very badly, breathing heavily and weakening.*

[63]

Soundtrack:)
'. . . For this day in Bethlehem is born unto you a Saviour,
which is Christ the Lord.'
(*Cut to:*)

INT. JUNIOR SCHOOL. DAY
*Close-up of three silver halos nodding and quivering across frame left
to right. Pan with them.*
Soundtrack:
CHILDREN'S CHOIR: (*Singing*) 'Oh come let us adore Him!
　　　Oh come let us adore Him!'
　　(*Cut to:*)

INT. JUNIOR SCHOOL CLASSROOM. DAY
*Front shot. Tableau. The climax of the school nativity play. The three
angels (young* TUCKER *is the middle one), their wings and halos
quivering, their hands joined, enter shot, very embarrassed. They
arrange themselves behind the Holy Family by standing on chairs.*
Soundtrack:
CHILDREN'S CHOIR: (*Singing*) 'Oh come let us adore Him!
　　　Christ the Lord!'
　　(*Cut to mid-shot of three boys. They have false beards on and
　　each carries a gift. They are the* THREE WISE MEN. *They walk
　　towards camera.*)
THREE WISE MEN: (*Singing*) 'We three Kings of Orient are,
　　　Bearing gifts we travel so far . . .'
　　(*Cut to front shot. Tableau. Holy Family and angels.* THREE
　　WISE MEN *enter left.*)
THREE WISE MEN: (*Singing*) 'Field and fountain,
　　　Moor and mountain,
　　　Following yonder star . . .'
　　(*And an angel with a silver star on a stick moves across frame to
　　left of Holy Family. The* THREE WISE MEN *kneel to baby
　　Jesus.*)
ALL: (*Singing*) 'Oh star of wonder, star of night,
　　　Star of royal beauty bright . . .'
　　(*The* THREE WISE MEN *present their gifts.*)
ALL: (*Singing*) 'Westward leading,
　　　Still proceeding,

[64]

Guide us with thy perfect light.'
(*Cut to:*)

INT. JUNIOR SCHOOL CLASSROOM WINDOW. DAY
Pan along window right to left.
Soundtrack:
CHILDREN'S CHOIR: (*Singing*) 'Away in a manger no crib for a
    bed,
    The little Lord Jesus lays down
    His sweet head . . .'
(*Continue panning. The window has been decorated with cotton
snow and Christmas scenes.*
*Dissolve to pan right to left to the school crib, the Holy Family
mounted on straw.*
Soundtrack:)
'The stars in the bright sky
  looked down where he lay,
The little Lord Jesus
  asleep on the hay . . .'
(*Dissolve to:*)

INT. GERIATRIC WARD. EVENING
Close-up of star on top of ward Christmas tree.
Soundtrack:
CHILDREN'S CHOIR: (*Singing*) 'The cattle are lowing,
    the baby awakes . . .'
(*Pan slowly down tree right to left. Two nurses dressing tree.*
FIRST NURSE, *standing on a set of steps, is on the right of the
tree, dressing it.* SECOND NURSE, *to the left of tree, is handing
small Christmas ornaments to* FIRST NURSE.
Soundtrack:)
CHILDREN'S CHOIR: (*Singing*) 'The little Lord Jesus
    no crying he makes . . .'
(*The two* NURSES *talk softly. Pan down tree right to left until*
SECOND NURSE *is framed in medium close-up, bottom left.*)
SECOND NURSE: (*Continuing to hand ornaments to* FIRST NURSE)
    I love Christmas Eve . . . don't you, Staff?
(*Pan away from her right to left.*
Soundtrack:)

[65]

CHILDREN'S CHOIR: (*Singing*) 'Be near me Lord Jesus
    Look down from the sky . . .'
(Dissolve to pan right to left until old TUCKER *is framed in
close-up, head on, in bed. He looks very weak.
Soundtrack:)*
CHILDREN'S CHOIR: (*Singing*) 'And stay by my side
    until morning is nigh.'
*(Hold close-up.
Cut to long shot of ward from sister's desk end. The two* NURSES
walk towards camera as they go off duty.)
TWO NURSES: Good night . . . All the best lads . . .
*(They exit. Then one by one the night nurse switches off the ward
lights. Darkness. Pause.
Soundtrack:)*
PRIEST: (*Voice over*) And the glory of the Lord shone, round
    about them, and they were sore afraid.
*(Hold.
Cut to:)*

INT. GERIATRIC WARD. NIGHT

*Long shot of ward from Christmas tree end looking up towards sister's
desk. Pause. Then the night* NURSE *gets up from the desk. She wears
a cape and carries a torch, which she switches on.
Soundtrack:)*
CHOIR: (*Singing*) 'Silent night, Holy night,
    All is calm, all is bright . . .'
*(She begins walking along the beds, shining the torch on the faces
of the patients to see if they are asleep.
Cut to track along first row of beds right to left –* NURSE'S *point
of view. Torch shining on sleeping faces.
Soundtrack:)*
    'Round yon Virgin, Mother and Child
    Holy infant so tender and mild . . .'
(Dissolve to track along second row of beds right to left –
NURSE'S *point of view. Torch shining on the patients.
Soundtrack:)*
    'Sleep in heavenly peace,
    Sleep in heavenly peace.'
(Fade singing. Track stops when TUCKER *is framed from the*

*foot of his bed. Torchlight on his face. His eyes flicker open, then
close. He is obviously very ill.
Cut to:)*

INT. CHURCH

*Low angled shot of huge crucifix.
Soundtrack:*

OLD TUCKER: *(Voice over)* Oh sacred heart of Jesus I give you my
body and blood . . .
(Cut to:)

INT. GERIATRIC WARD. NIGHT

High-angled shot of old TUCKER *in bed.* NURSE *goes to him and
examines him for a moment.
Soundtrack:*

OLD TUCKER: *(Voice over)* Oh sacred heart of Jesus I give you,
my heart and my soul . . .
(Cut to:)

INT. CHURCH

*Close-up of the sacristy light. A candle burns low in it.
Soundtrack:*

OLD TUCKER: *(Voice over)* When the light goes out – God is dead.
(Cut to:)

INT. GERIATRIC WARD. NIGHT

Mid shot side view of TUCKER'*s silhouette in bed.* NURSE *leaning
over him. She switches off the torch. Then she moves back towards the
end of the bed and sits in a chair. They are both in silhouette.
Soundtrack:*

NURSE: *(Voice over)* They know when they're going – you go and
sit by them but they know they're going.
*(The sound of rain can be heard very loudly. Hold.
Cut to:)*

INT. TUCKER'S CHILDHOOD HOME. LATE AFTERNOON

*Close-up of window. Through the window it is pouring with rain. Pan
down right to left away from the window across the room which is light
only by firelight.*

Continue pan past a small natural Christmas tree hung with ornaments, past and along a sideboard filled with Christmas cards and fruit. And in the centre of the sideboard a photograph of MOTHER *when she was younger, about thirty-five. Continue pan until* TUCKER *as a boy is framed. He is asleep on the hearthrug. Toys are scattered about him. Everything glows in the firelight. And over all this, the continuous sound of the heavy rain.*
Cut to:

INT. JUNIOR SCHOOL. DAY

The HEADMISTRESS's *study. Medium long shot of* HEADMISTRESS *from* TUCKER's *point of view as a boy.* TUCKER *however is not visible. The study is big, gloomy and over-furnished. The* HEADMISTRESS – *a nun* – *is seated at her desk, her back to the window. Through the window it is pouring with rain. As the room is lit only from the window the* HEADMISTRESS *appears in silhouette, making her appear like a shadow, a hooded figure whose features cannot be seen. Silence.*

HEADMISTRESS: Do you love God Robert?

TUCKER: (*As a boy, voice over*) Yes Sister.

    (*Cut to:*)

INT. GERIATRIC WARD. NIGHT

Long shot of old TUCKER *in bed* – *side view* – *from far end of the ward. His bed is lit by a white light coming in through a window directly opposite his bed. The light begins to flood in, making Tucker's bed appear to be the only object in the ward. Slowly track on* TUCKER *in his bed.*

Soundtrack: MOTHER *singing unaccompanied 'You're Still the Only Boy in the World'.*

TUCKER *begins to suffer great difficulty in breathing* – *long breaths getting progressively shallow* – *Cheyne Stokes breathing. This gets louder as we get closer. Continue track.*

Soundtrack: MOTHER *singing unaccompanied.*

Continue track. We are now close enough to see TUCKER's *hands and arms rise slowly from the counterpane. Continue Cheyne Stokes breathing.*

Soundtrack:

MOTHER: (*Voice over singing unaccompanied*) 'My love for you

will ever be true . . .'
(*Dissolve to:*)

INT. WINDOW

Medium long shot of a young man standing naked at the window, his back to camera. The light floods in through the window. Track slowly in on him.
Soundtrack: continue Cheyne Stokes breathing. MOTHER *singing. The young man half turns towards camera and smiles.*
Dissolve to:

INT. GERIATRIC WARD. NIGHT

Close-shot side view of TUCKER *in bed, his hands reaching towards the light. Continue Cheyne Stokes breathing. Crab around to front of bed, then track back away from* TUCKER, *his hands reaching towards the light which is getting brighter all the time. Continue Cheyne Stokes breathing.*
Soundtrack: MOTHER *singing unaccompanied 'You're Still the Only Boy in the World'.*
Dissolve to close shot of the window opposite TUCKER's *bed. The light pours in, getting brighter still. Track in on it. Continue Cheyne Stokes breathing.*
Soundtrack:)
MOTHER: (*Voice over, singing unaccompanied*) 'The one and only boy for me . . .'
　　　(*The light gets brighter. The Cheyne Stokes breathing more difficult and rapid, then suddenly it cuts out.*
　　　Light. Continue track. Silence. A momentary pause. Then fade to black.)

Distant Voices, Still Lives

The cast and crew of *Distant Voices, Still Lives* included:

MOTHER	Freda Dowie
FATHER	Pete Postlethwaite
EILEEN	Angela Walsh
TONY	Dean Williams
MAISIE	Lorraine Ashbourne
EILEEN as a child	Sally Davies
TONY as a child	Nathan Walsh
MAISIE as a child	Susan Flanagan
MICKY	Debi Jones
RED	Chris Darwin
JINGLES	Marie Jelliman
LES	Andrew Schofield
GRANNY	Anny Dyson
AUNTY NELL	Jean Boht
DOREEN	Pauline Quirke
MR SPAULL	Matthew Long
MARGIE	Frances Dell
UNCLE TED	Roy Ford
Written and Directed by	Terence Davies
Producer	Jennifer Howarth
Executive Producer	Colin MacCabe
Photography and Editing	William Diver
Photography	Patrick Duval
Costume Designer	Monica Howe
Art Directors	Miki van Zwanenberg
	Jocelyn James

A British Film Institute Production, in association with Channel 4 and ZDF, 1988.

Distant Voices

NB:

Distant Voices is about memory and the mosaic of memory.

Father is the central pivot around which Mother, Eileen, Maisie and Tony revolve and all have equal dramatic weight.

Memory does not move in a linear or a chronological way – its pattern is of a circular nature, placing events (not in their 'natural' or 'real' order) but recalled for their emotional importance.

Memory *is* its own validity.

Thus any 'story' involving memory is not a narrative in the conventional sense but of necessity more diffuse, more elliptical. Therefore conventional narrative expectation will not be satisfied in any conventional way, and I would ask you to bear this in mind when you are reading this piece.

I was trying to create 'a pattern of timeless moments'.

Blackness.
Fade up main title 'Distant Voices'. *Sound of rain and thunder.*
Fade out main title.
Fade up to:

EXT. MORNING. MID-1950S
A terraced house. Rain. Thunder.
VOICE OVER: (*1950s BBC Radio announcer*) 'Faroes, Cromarty,
Forth, Tyne . . .'
>   (MOTHER *opens the front door, picks up the milk, looks up and
>   down the street, then closes the front door. Cut to:*)

INT. MORNING. MID-1950S
Hallway and stairs as seen from the front door.
MOTHER *walks down the hallway (away from camera) and stops at
the foot of the stairs.*
MOTHER: (*Calling softly*) It's seven o'clock you three!
>   (*Walks away to kitchen.*)
VOICE OVER: (*1950s BBC Radio announcer*) 'Dogger, German
Bight, Rockall, Mallin, Hebrides, Fastnet . . .'
>   (MOTHER *walks back up the hall to the foot of the stairs.*)
MOTHER: Eileen! Tony! Maisie!
>   You'd better get your skates on!
>   (*She exits down hall.*
>   *Hold on empty hall and stairs.*
>   *Soundtrack of* MOTHER's *voice over, singing* 'I Get the Blues
>   When It's Raining'.
>   *BBC Radio* 'Lift up your Hearts'.
>   *Footsteps on the empty stairs.*)
TONY: (*Voice over*) Morning Mam.
MOTHER: (*Voice over*) Are those two sisters of yours up yet,
>   Tony?
TONY: (*Voice over*) Yer – they're just coming down.
MAISIE: (*Voice over*) Hi yer Mam.
MOTHER: (*Voice over*) Morning Maisie.
EILEEN: (*Voice over*) Morning Mam.
MOTHER: (*Voice over*) Morning Eileen.

[75]

Nervous love?

EILEEN: (*Voice over*) A bit.

MOTHER: (*Voice over*) Have a cuppa and a ciggie.

(*Track around 180 degrees and crane up from this camera position until the front door (which is closed) is framed.*
Hallway and door as seen from the stairs. Voice over of MOTHER *singing 'I Get the Blues When It's Raining' continues.*
From the same camera position the front door opens in a dissolve.
Sunshine. Through the front door a hearse is seen drawing up (right to left), early 1950s.
Soundtrack of Jessye Norman singing, voice over 'There's a Man Goin' Round Takin' Names'.
Dissolve to:)

PARLOUR. EARLY 1950S. MORNING. FUNERAL

Tableau. Family group. MOTHER *flanked by* TONY *on one side and* EILEEN *and* MAISIE *on the other. All in black. Above them on the wall a photograph of* FATHER. TONY *and* MAISIE *grim.* MOTHER *and* EILEEN *tearful.*
Soundtrack, Jessye Norman singing 'There's a Man Goin' Round Takin' Names'.
They all stand. Track in on them. They all walk towards camera and exit.
Keep tracking until photograph of father is framed in close-up. He is smiling and holding on to a horse.
Hold. Dissolve to:

INT. MORNING. EARLY 1950S. FUNERAL

Camera position as at opening – from front door looking down hallway to stairs.
The family group entering shot.
They stand for a moment.
Dissolve to family funeral group seen through the bannisters.
They walk down the hall towards the front door.
Pan with them.
Soundtrack, voice over of Jessye Norman singing 'There's a Man Goin' Round Takin' Names' continues.

Front door closes.
Hold. Cut to:

INT. PARLOUR. AFTERNOON. WEDDING GROUP.
MID-1950S

Tableaux. EILEEN (*the bride*) *flanked by* TONY (*on her right*),
MOTHER *and* MAISIE *standing at the back of them.*
They all wear buttonholes. All smiling nervously.
Soundtrack, voice over of Jessye Norman singing, continues.
Track in on EILEEN. *Track stops when* EILEEN *and* TONY *are in*
two-shot, close-up.

EILEEN: (*To* TONY, *who smiles uneasily*) I wish me Dad was here.
(*Pause.*
Pan to MAISIE.
MAISIE *in close-up, looking grim.*)

MAISIE: (*Voice over*) I don't. He was a bastard and I bleedin' hated
him!
(*Cut to:*)

INT. HOSPITAL WARD. DAY. EARLY 1950S

Long shot of ward. Beds running down the long ward. MOTHER,
EILEEN, MAISIE *and* TONY (*in army uniform*) *walking down towards*
father's bed.

MOTHER: (*Voice over*) They had to stretch his gullet.
(*The group stop at father's bed and look down at him. Favour*
MAISIE *in this shot.*
Cut to shot of FATHER *in bed from group's point of view. He is*
very frail and ill.)

MAISIE: (*Voice over*) Can I have the money to go to the dance, Dad?

FATHER: (*Voice over*) You get that cellar done – never mind
bleedin' dances.

MAISIE: (*Voice over*) But Dad, there's rats down there – I'm
terrified of rats.

FATHER: (*Voice over, furious*) No cellar – no dance!
(*Cut to:*)

INT. CELLAR. AFTERNOON. EARLY 1950S

Medium long shot. Stone-flagged cellar. MAISIE *kneeling scrubbing the*
flags.

[77]

FATHER *walks across behind her kneeling figure.*
MAISIE *stops scrubbing.*
MAISIE: Can I go to the dance, Dad?
> (*He just throws the money on to the floor. She leans across and picks it up.*
> *Cut to close-up of* MAISIE.)
MAISIE: (*With as much sarcasm as she can muster*) Thanks.
> (*Cut to shot of* FATHER *from* MAISIE's *point of view.*
> *He picks up a yard brush and turns on her in a fury.*)
FATHER: You're just like your Aunty May and she was no bleedin' good!
> (*He begins to rain blow after blow down on* MAISIE *with the yard brush. She is screaming.*
> *Soundtrack: carry her screaming over the next shot, as we cut back to:*)

INT. PARLOUR. DAY. MID-1950S. WEDDING GROUP
Two-shot of EILEEN *and* TONY.
EILEEN: I wish me Dad was here.
> (*Pan to* TONY. TONY *in close-up. He looks at her. Hold.*
> *Cut to:*)

INT. PARLOUR. NIGHT. EARLY 1950S
Close shot of windows.
Suddenly they are smashed from the outside – hands repeatedly coming in and out of the panes. TONY *is smashing the windows with his bare hands.* TONY *is now seen through the smashed windows. He is in army uniform, and is shouting in a paroxysm of rage and years of hurt.*
TONY: Come out and fight me you bastard! Come out and fight me you bastard!
> (*He is now crying with fury and anger, his voice hoarse.*)
> Come out and fight me! YOU BASTARD! Come out and *Fight!*
> (*Over and over again.*
> *Cut to medium close-up of* TONY *in uniform.*)
> (*Pleading*) Will you have a drink with me, Dad?
> (*Cut to medium close-up of* FATHER *at fireside.*)
FATHER: (*Unmoved*) No.
> (*Cut to medium close-up of* MOTHER.)

[78]

MOTHER: (*Begging*) Have a drink with him, Tommy . . . Please.
  (*Cut to two-shot – mid-long – of* TONY (*left of frame standing*)
  and FATHER (*right of frame sitting at fireside*).
  TONY's *hands covered in blood. He is holding bottles of pale ale
  and Double Diamond.*)
FATHER: (*Angry*) I said No.
TONY: (*Taking two old pennies from his pocket and throwing them
  into the fire*) Tuppence – that's all I've got.
  (*Throws coins into fire.*)
  But I wouldn't give *you* daylight.
  (*Cut to medium shot (side view) of* FATHER *at fireside.
  He picks up the poker and prods the pennies deeper into the fire.
  Cut to:*)

EXT. STREET. NIGHT. EARLY 1950S

TONY *being bundled into a van by several military policemen.
He starts to resist, then fight.
They begin to really beat him up as they manhandle him into the van.
Cut to:*

INT. CORRIDOR OF GUARDHOUSE. NIGHT. EARLY 1950S

*High shot looking down corridor. Cells on either side of corridor. Grills
in doors.
A face comes to a door grill on right-hand side of corridor.*
MAN: (*At cell-door grill*) Play 'Limelight', Scouse.
  (*Cut to:*)

INT. TONY'S CELL. NIGHT. EARLY 1950S

*Tony sitting on a bed (with no mattress). He bangs his harmonica on
his thigh then begins softly to play 'Limelight'.
Cut to:*

INT. GUARDHOUSE CORRIDOR. NIGHT. EARLY 1950S

*High shot.
The sound of the harmonica.*
2ND MAN: (*Voice over*) Go on, Scouse . . . Give us a tune.
  (*Soundtrack: The sound of the harmonica being played into next
  shot.
  Cut to:*)

INT. TRAIN. DAY. EARLY 1950S

Train travelling right to left.

TONY *in two shot with another soldier.*

Soundtrack: Cross-fade 'Limelight' with TONY *going through the list of heavyweight boxing champions from earliest times to the present day.*

SOLDIER: It was Schmelling, Scouse . . .

TONY: You're wrong – Schmelling never won the title . . . the heavyweight champions were Jack Sharkey, Primo Carnera, Braddock, Baer – no, I tell a lie . . . Baer *then* Braddock then Joe Louis who held it from 1937 to 1948 and then –

2ND SOLDIER: Come on Scouse . . .

> (*Begins to sing 'It Takes a Worried Man to Sing a Worried Song'. They all join in.*
> *Cut to:*)

INT. PARLOUR. NIGHT. EARLY 1950S

MOTHER *and* TONY *in two shot close-up, side view.*

MOTHER: Thanks for coming home, son.

TONY: I got compassionate leave, Mam.

> (*Cut to:*)

INT. HOSPITAL WARD. DAY. EARLY 1950S

Close-up of FATHER, *very ill.*

FATHER: I was wrong, lad.

> (*Cut to close-up of* TONY *standing in army uniform by foot of the bed.*)

TONY: OK, Dad. OK.

> (*Dissolve:*)

EXT. STREET. DAY. EARLY 1950S. FUNERAL

Mid shot of front doorstep and hall.

Funeral group comes to the doorstep and stands there, MOTHER *and* TONY, *and behind them* EILEEN *and* MAISIE.

A small group of neighbours on either side of the door watch them. Pause.

A passenger car pulls up in front of them. Left to right, they enter it. Cut to:

[80]

INT. HALLWAY. DAY. EARLY 1950S. FUNERAL
Funeral group walking down steps and into the passenger car. It moves off, right to left.
Cut to:

INT. PARLOUR. AFTERNOON. MID-1950S. WEDDING
Tableaux shot of wedding group, all nerves.
TONY: Are you ready, Ei?
EILEEN: Here goes.
   (*Cut to:*)

INT. CHURCH. DAY. MID-1950S
Close-up of two pairs of hands. EILEEN *and her husband-to-be. He puts the ring on her finger.*
Priest's voice over intoning the Wedding Service.
Cut to:

INT. KITCHEN. EARLY SUMMER EVENING. MID-1950S
Close-up of EILEEN, *side view.*
EILEEN: (*Unbelieving*) Look what he's bought me.
   (*Cut to close-up of* JINGLES, *side view.*)
JINGLES: (*Awestruck*) It's Chanel No. 5!
EILEEN: (*Voice over*) I know.
   (*Cut to close-up of* MONICA, *threequarter side view.*)
MONICA: (*Absolutely overcome as she puts her elbows on the table and cradles her face in her hands*) Oh . . . isn't that *dead* romantic!
   (*Cut to wide shot of all three girls just sitting looking at the bottle of Chanel which is on the kitchen table.*
   Cut to:)

INT. HALLWAY. DAY. MID-1950S. EILEEN'S WEDDING
Mid-long shot of street through open front door. Passenger car pulls up left to right.
EILEEN *and* DAVE *get out of the car and come into the house. Neighbours throw confetti.*
EILEEN *and* DAVE *smiling as they come indoors, followed by* MOTHER, MAISIE *and* TONY *and other relatives and guests.*
Cut to:

[81]

INT. PARLOUR. DAY. MID-1950S. EILEEN'S WEDDING
Mid-wide shot of table in front of window.
EILEEN *and* DAVE *in centre. Their wedding cake in front of them. They are flanked by* MOTHER *and* MAISIE *on their right and* TONY *on their left.* EILEEN *and* DAVE *stand and pose to cut the cake. All hold still. Silence.*
Photographer takes a flash photo. All relax. Applause. Laughter. Dissolve to:

INT. PUB. NIGHT. MID-1950S. EILEEN'S WEDDING
Pan around from left to right the smiling, singing faces.
They are finishing a song. Singing 'If You Knew Suzie'.
Pan stops on MAISIE, *who begins to sing solo 'My Yiddisher Momma'.*
Cut to two shot of EILEEN *and* TONY.
EILEEN: (*Crying, howling like an animal*) I WANT MY DAD!
　　(TONY *holding her. Both weeping.*)
　　I want my dad . . .
　　(*She cries and wails. He weeps.*
　　Soundtrack, voice over of MAISIE *singing 'My Yiddisher Momma'.*
　　Cross fade to:)
CHOIR: (*Voice over, singing*) 'In the bleak mid-winter
　　　　Frosty winds made moan,
　　　　Earth stood hard as iron
　　　　Water like a stone . . .'
　　(*Track, right to left, away from* EILEEN *and* TONY *into the darkness of the street.*
　　It starts to snow.)
EILEEN: (*Voice over*) I know me Dad was bad – I know that – but I
　　always try and think of the good times – like Christmas.
CHOIR: (*Voice over, singing*) 'Snow had fallen, snow on snow
　　　　Snow on snow,
　　　　In the bleak mid-winter
　　　　Long ago . . .'
　　(*Dissolve to:*)

INT. BEDROOM. NIGHT. EARLY 1940S
Continue tracking, right to left, to side view of a home-made altar/crib in blackness.

[82]

Candles and night lights being lit by five pairs of hands.
Continue tracking as EILEEN, TONY, MAISIE *as children and*
MOTHER *and* FATHER *(kneeling behind them) come into view. They*
are lighting the candles. All are radiant.
Soundtrack:
CHOIR: (*Voice over, singing*) 'Our God, Heaven cannot hold him
　　　　Nor Earth sustain; Heaven and Earth shall flee away,
　　　　When he comes to reign; . . .'
　　　(*Dissolve to:*)

EXT. STREET. NIGHT. EARLY 1940S

Continue tracking, right to left, over the exteriors of the houses. Through
the windows parlours that have been dressed for Christmas can be seen.
Soundtrack:
EILEEN:
MAISIE: } (*Voices over – as children*) If I should die before I wake,
TONY:
　　　　Pray the Lord my soul to take.
　　　　God bless Mother,
　　　　God bless Father,
　　　　And keep them safe.
CHOIR: (*Voice over, singing*) 'In the bleak mid-winter
　　　　A stable place sufficed
　　　　The Lord God Almighty
　　　　Jesus Christ . . .'
　　　(*Track stops at third window.*
　　　Through it FATHER *can be seen decorating a small Christmas tree*
　　　which is on the sideboard, his back to camera.
　　　Soundtrack:)
CHOIR: (*Voice over, singing*) 'Enough for him, whom cherubim
　　　　Worship night and day,
　　　　A breast full of milk,
　　　　And a manger full of hay;
　　　　Enough for him, whom angels
　　　　Fall down before,
　　　　The ox and the ass and camel
　　　　Which adore . . .'
　　　(*Dissolve to* FATHER (*still with back to camera*) *as he finishes*
　　　dressing the Christmas tree.)

[83]

MOTHER: (*Voice over*) Say goodnight to your Dad.
   (FATHER *turns and smiles.*
   Cut to shot of MOTHER *with* EILEEN, TONY *and* MAISIE *as children, ready for bed.*)
EILEEN:
TONY: } (*As children*) Goodnight, Dad.
MAISIE:
FATHER: (*Voice over*) Goodnight kids.
   (MOTHER *and children exit.*
   Soundtrack:)
CHOIR: (*Voice over, singing*) 'Angels and Archangels
      May have gathered there
      Cherubim and seraphim
      Thronged the air . . .'
(*Cut to* FATHER *at sideboard turning back to the Christmas tree.*
Soundtrack:)
MOTHER: (*Voice over*) Come on – up the dancers!
   (*Children giggling as they go upstairs.*
   Cut to:)

INT. CHILDREN'S BEDROOM. NIGHT. EARLY 1940S
Pan with FATHER, *in close-up, creeping into bedroom.*
Cut to the three children sleeping in the bed, pan to them.
CHOIR: (*Voice over, singing*) 'But only his mother
      In her maiden bliss
      Worshipped the Beloved
      With a kiss . . .'
(FATHER *places three Christmas stockings on the end of the bed.*
Cut to FATHER *in close-up.* FATHER *looking down at the sleeping children with love. His eyes fill with tears.*)
FATHER: (*Very softly*) God bless.
CHOIR: (*Voice over, singing*) 'What can I give him
      Poor as I am?
      If I were a shepherd
      I would bring a lamb . . .'
   (*Cut to:*)

INT. KITCHEN. NIGHT. EARLY 1940S

Shot of table.

FATHER *at the head of the table.* MAISIE *as a child to his right –*
TONY *and* EILEEN, *as children, to his left.*

Soundtrack carol climaxes:

CHOIR: (*Voice over, singing*) 'If I were a Wise Man
     I would do my part;
     Yet what can I give him –
     Give my heart.'

    (FATHER *rises in a fury.*
    The table is laden with Christmas food.
    Suddenly he grabs the tablecloth and drags everything off the
    table.)

FATHER: (*In a fury*) NELLIE! CLEAN IT UP!
    (*Cut to:*)

INT. BEDROOM. NIGHT. EARLY 1940S

Pitch blackness.

Soundtrack:

EILEEN: (*As a child, very ill*) What's scarlet fever, Mam?

MOTHER: (*Quietly*) It's scarlettina, love. Scarlettina . . .
    (EILEEN, *lying in bed in foreground, gradually comes into*
    focus.)
    (*From the bedroom door*) How are you Ei?

EILEEN: (*Weakly*) I'm OK Mam.
    (MOTHER *comes to bed and sits down.*
    She begins to stroke EILEEN'*s hair.*
    Clearly she is upset.
    Silence.)
    Where's our Tony, Mam?
    (MOTHER *doesn't answer.*
    Cut to:)

EXT. STREET. NIGHT. EARLY 1940S

Back view of TONY *as a child.*

Front door opens.

FATHER *standing there.*

TONY: (*As a child*) Why can't I come in, Dad?

FATHER: There's no place for you here – frigg off!

(*Slams door in* TONY's *face.*
Cut to side view close-up of TONY *as a child.*
He just stands there trying to prevent himself from crying.
He looks up at the bedroom window.
Cut to MOTHER *at the bedroom window from* TONY's *point of view.*
She just stands there in tears, shaking her head.
Cut to back view of TONY *as a child.*
Pause.
He backs away from the front door and moves left. Pan with him. As he walks slowly down the street he puts his hands into his pockets then breaks into a trot.)

TONY: (*As a child, voice over*) Can I stay here, Gran?
GRANNY: (*Voice over*) You can have the sofa.
      (*Cut to:*)

INT. PARLOUR. NIGHT. MID-1950S. EILEEN'S WEDDING
Close-up of Aunty Nell singing 'Roll Along Kentucky Moon'.
AUNTY NELL: More band!
      (*Pan away from her, left to right.*)
GRANNY: (*Voice over*) Whoopie!
      (*Pan to* GRANNY *when she is in close-up.*
      Pan to GRANNY. *When she is in close-up pan stops.*
      GRANNY *sings 'A Little Bit of Cucumber'.*)
AUNTY NELL: (*Voice over*) More bleedin' band.
      (*Pan away to* MONICA *in close-up, left to right.*)
MONICA: Your Gran's in fine feckle.
      (*Continue pan to* EILEEN, *in close-up.*)
EILEEN: Yer – she's just come back from the Isle of Man.
      (*Continue pan to* MAISIE, *in close-up.*)
MAISIE: She should've stayed there – the auld cow – she's just like me Dad and I bleedin' hate her.
      (*Cut to:*)

INT. NIGHT. 1940S
Medium close-up of EILEEN, MAISIE *and* TONY *as children, their backs to camera but their faces seen in reflection in a mirror. Complete darkness surrounds them.*
They are illuminated by a single nightlight in front of the mirror.

[86]

GRANNY: (*Voice over*) If you look into a mirror after midnight –
you'll see the devil.
(*Her face looms up out of the blackness and appears disembodied
above them in the mirror. They are terrified.*
GRANNY *half laughs, half grins.*
Cut to:)

INT. STABLE. DAY. LATE 1940S

Close-up of FATHER. *He is seen across the back of a horse which he is
curry-combing.*
Cut to EILEEN, MAISIE *and* TONY *as children, painstakingly
climbing a ladder which leads to a hayloft. They make no noise. Crane
up with them. They reach the straw-filled loft and crawl commando-
style across it.*
FATHER: (*Voice over, half whistling, half singing*) 'Irish Eyes . . .'
(*The three children reach the edge of the loft.*
Track in with them and over them.
FATHER *seen in high shot, curry-combing the horse as he half
whistles, half sings.*
Cut to stable floor (FATHER'*s point of view*) *of hayloft.*
*Slowly – very slowly – their three faces appear over the edge of
the loft.*
They just look and listen as FATHER *continues half whistling,
half singing 'Irish Eyes'.*
Cut to:)

EXT. STREET. DAY. LATE 1940S

Low-angle shot from street of MOTHER *cleaning bedroom windows.
She sits on the outside window ledge with her legs inside the room.*
Cut to high shot of MAISIE *from* MOTHER'*s point of view, walking
towards camera and looking up at the bedroom window.*
MAISIE: (*As a child, voice over*) Don't fall, Mam – *Please* don't
fall.
(*Dissolve to:*)

INT. LANDING. DAY. LATE 1940S

Mid-shot, low-angle, of EILEEN *and* TONY *as children, their faces
appearing and looking round banister towards camera.*

[87]

INT. BEDROOM. DAY. LATE 1940S

Long shot of bedroom window, the rest of the room dark but one or two objects catching the light: a corner of a bed, a little chest of drawers . . . Sun blazing through the window, curtains billowing softly.
Right of the window, on the floor, a bucket.
Only MOTHER's *legs and feet can be seen as she sits on the outside of the window-ledge washing the windows. As she does so she is almost obliterated by the sun.*
Very slowly track in on her.
Soundtrack:
MAISIE: (*As an adult, voice over*) Why did you marry him, Mam?
MOTHER: (*Voice over*) He was nice, he was a good dancer.
    (*Voice over of Ella Fitzgerald singing 'Taking a Chance on Love'.*
    Dissolve/cut to:)

INT. PARLOUR AND HALL. DAY. EARLY 1950S

A continuous tracking two shot of MOTHER *and* FATHER *in parlour then ending in the hall.*
He is beating her relentlessly and she is screaming.
MOTHER: Tommy! Tommy! Oh stop Tommy! Stop!
    (*Soundtrack of Ella Fitzgerald voice over singing 'Taking a Chance on Love'.*
    FATHER *walks away back down the hall to parlour, leaving* MOTHER's *crumpled body on the floor.*
    Hold.
    Only her moans can be heard.
    Soundtrack of Ella Fitzgerald voice over singing 'Taking a Chance on Love'.
    Cut to:)

INT. PARLOUR. DAY. EARLY 1950S

Close-up of MOTHER's *face, side view. It is almost unrecognizable – like a boxer's after a particularly vicious fight. She is trying not to cry but clearly every movement is agony. She is polishing the sideboard. Blood trickles down from her nose and mouth and drips on to the sideboard. Pan down to top of sideboard. Blood drips on to the surface and* MOTHER *continues slowly to rub the polish and the blood into the surface of the wood.*
Cut to:

INT. COAL-HOLE IN CELLAR. DAY. EARLY 1950S

MAISIE *as an adult in coal-hole, shovelling coal into a bucket. She is lit only from above, from the pin-points of light coming in through the overhead iron coal-hole lid.*

She stops shovelling coal and looks up into the light.

MAISIE: (*In a quiet voice filled with impotent rage and furious hatred*)
  If anything happens to my Mam I'll bleedin' kill you!

TONY: (*Voice over*) Go on Ma – give us 'Barefoot Days'.
  (*Dissolve to:*)

INT. PARLOUR. NIGHT. MID-1950S.
EILEEN'S WEDDING

Close-up of MOTHER*'s hands. As she begins to sing her hands beat time on her lap.* MOTHER *sings 'Barefoot Days'.*
Pan slowly up to her smiling face. She continues to sing.
She is now in close-up.
Guests begin to join in.
Pan slowly, from left to right, around the happy singing faces until EILEEN, TONY *and* MAISIE *are framed. They are singing too.*
Dissolve:

INT. CELLAR. DAY. 1940

Continue panning shot, left to right.
FATHER, MOTHER, EILEEN, MAISIE, TONY, *as children, chopping wood and putting it into bundles.*
Soundtrack of voice over singing 'Barefoot Days' continues.
Pan ends.
Cut to tableau shot of entire family.
Soundtrack of voice over singing 'Barefoot Days' continues.
Silence.
They all continue chopping and bundling wood and putting it into piles.
Cut to:

EXT. ALLEY. DAY. 1940

EILEEN, MAISIE *and* TONY *as children, pushing a handcart laden with wood.*
Soundtrack: air-raid siren starts. They run faster with the cart.
Air-raid siren wails louder. They stop running and get under the cart.

[89]

Cut to close-up of the three children under the cart.
Soundtrack: distant planes, sirens, bombs.
Cut to:

INT. AIR-RAID SHELTER. DAY. 1940
Soundtrack: sirens and distant bombs.
Close shot: MOTHER *and* FATHER *in the midst of the crowd being pushed into the air-raid shelter by the crowd's momentum.*
MOTHER: (*Frantic*) Where are the kids, Tommy? Where are the
    kids?
    (*Cut to:*)

EXT. STREET. DAY. 1940
High shot. A parade of shops.
EILEEN, MAISIE, TONY *as children running past them, right to left, followed by an ARP warden.*
Soundtrack: bombs, aircraft swooping down suddenly.
Cut to planes' point of view, swooping down and shattering the shop windows with tracer bullets.
Cut to:

EXT. SHOP DOORWAY. DAY. 1940
The children and ARP warden crashing to the ground inside shop doorway, glass showering them.
Soundtrack: bombs. Planes drone away.
Cut to:

AIR-RAID SHELTER. DAY. 1940
Close-up of FATHER.
Soundtrack: bombs getting progressively louder and closer.
FATHER: (*Furious*) Where the bleedin' hell have you been?
    (*Cut to three shot of children,* EILEEN *in front,* TONY *and*
    MAISIE *behind.* FATHER *slaps* EILEEN *right across the face. She
    is more stunned than hurt.*
    Soundtrack: bombs very loud. People begin to panic.)
FIRST VOICE OVER: They're getting closer.
SECOND VOICE OVER: They're gonna bomb us!
    (*Cut to four shot.* FATHER *facing camera. The children backs to
    camera.* EILEEN *is lifted up by* FATHER.

[90]

Cut to FATHER *holding* EILEEN *up. Mid-close up.*)
FATHER: Sing, Eileen! Sing!
(EILEEN *singing tentatively 'Roll Out the Barrel'.*
FATHER *joins in.*
Cut to wide shot or pan around, right to left.
One by one people join in – singing quietly and afraid.
Soundtrack: bombs very loud.
All sing 'Roll Out the Barrel'.)

INT. KITCHEN. EARLY SUMMER EVENING. EARLY 1950S
Mid three shot of EILEEN, MONICA *and* JINGLES *looking directly
into camera, as if it were a mirror. They are getting made up.*
JINGLES: Wo – oh – it's Saturday!
Yes! It's Sat – ur – day!
(*Soundtrack: on the radio, Guy Mitchell and Cindy Carson sing
'Cos I Love Ya that's a Why'.*
EILEEN, MONICA *and* JINGLES *finish getting made up, putting
lipstick on as they finish, pursing their lips.*)
MONICA: (*Wetting her forefingers and running them over her eyebrows
very quickly*) Oh kiss me you fool!
(*They all smile.*
A knock on the front door is heard.
Cut to:)
EILEEN: (*Gathering herself together somewhat nervously*) That's
him.
JINGLES: Bet he's come in a taxi.
MONICA: Well you know these seamen – money's no object.
(EILEEN *exits.*
Cut to:)

EXT. STREET. FRONT DOOR. EARLY SUMMER EVENING.
EARLY 1950S
Close-up of EILEEN *opening front door. She is horrified by what she
sees.*
EILEEN: (*More to herself than anything*) It's me Dad.
(*Cut to:*)

INT. HALLWAY. EARLY SUMMER EVENING. EARLY 1950S
Shot of FATHER *from* EILEEN'S *point of view.*

[91]

He is swaying on the doorstep. He is very, very ill – like a Belsen victim.

FATHER: I've signed meself out of hospital.

I've walked home.

(*He literally falls into the hall.*

Cut to:)

INT. PARLOUR. NIGHT. EARLY 1950S

Close-up of GRANNY.

GRANNY: (*In tears*) He's gone – my Tommy's gone . . .

(*Cut to shot of* MOTHER, EILEEN, MAISIE *and* TONY.

MOTHER *sits down in a chair.*

EILEEN *and* MAISIE *come and stand behind her.*

TONY *in a chair by the fireside, elbows on knees, lowers his head.*

They all look exhausted – more relieved than upset.

Cut to low-angled shot, side view, of FATHER'*s head on bed.*

Pennies on his eyes.

Hold.)

MONICA: (*Voice over*) Arh – he was all right, your dad.

EILEEN: (*Voice over*) You were the only one who could get around him.

(*Cut to close-up of a pair of boots on the sideboard.*)

MONICA: (*Voice over*) What'll you give me for them, Mr. D.?

(*Cut to close-up of* FATHER.)

FATHER: (*Roaring with laughter*) Micky, they're your dad's working boots!

(*Cut to close-up of* MONICA.)

MONICA: But we've just *got* to have five bob.

(*Cut to close-up of* FATHER.)

FATHER: (*Incredulous*) What for?

(*Cut to close-up of* EILEEN.)

EILEEN: Oh Dad we've just *got* to go to the dance.

(*Cut to close-up of* FATHER.)

FATHER: (*Disbelieving*) I don't know – you two are bleedin' dance mad.

(*Cut to close-up of* MONICA.)

MONICA: (*Pleading*) Arh – go on Mr D. Just five bob – don't be snidey.

(*Cut to close-up of* FATHER.)

[92]

FATHER: All right – I'll *lend* you the money – but take the boots
back home – OK?
(FATHER *throws her the money.*
Cut to mid-two shot of EILEEN *and* MONICA. MONICA *catches
the money.*)
MONICA: Arh – you're a pal, Mr D.
EILEEN: Thanks Dad!
(*Pan with them as they hurry out.*)
FATHER: (*Voice over*) And be back here by eleven!
(*Cut to close-up of* FATHER.)
FATHER: (*Still incredulous*) Bleedin' dance mad!
(*Cut to close-up of* MONICA *at the parlour door.*)
MONICA: How are we fixed for a few ciggies, Mr D.?
(*Cut to close-up of* FATHER.)
FATHER: (*Mock anger*) OUT!
(*Cut to:*)

EXT. STREET. NIGHT. EARLY 1950S
Shot of EILEEN *and* MONICA *sitting on doorstep with their best
dresses on.*
FATHER: (*Voice over from inside the house*) Eileen – it's nearly
eleven o'clock.
EILEEN: OK, Dad.
MONICA: (*Coaxing*) Just one last ciggie, Mr D.
EILEEN: I'll only be a minute Dad.
(*To* MONICA) You'll get me hung you will.
(EILEEN *gives* MONICA *a cigarette and has one herself. They
light up. Pause.*)
FATHER: (*Voice over*) Eileen – I won't tell you twice.
MONICA: (*Shouting back and coaxing*) Just a few more minutes and
she'll be in – honest –
FATHER: (*Voice over*) Make sure it is only a few minutes and all.
(*Silence as they savour their cigarettes.*)
MONICA: I'm sure I'm getting a brain tumour.
EILEEN: Oh Micky, behave! You're healthier than I am.
MONICA: No – honest kid – my head's been banging for days and –
FATHER: (*Voice over, roaring*) Eileen! What bleedin' time do you
call this!
(EILEEN *and* MONICA *frightened out of their wits.*)

[93]

EILEEN: (*Choking on her cigarette*) Oh God blimey! (*Shouting in*)
    I'm coming Dad! I'm coming!
MONICA: Isn't it terrible the way we've got to be in by eleven
    o'clock?
EILEEN: I know. It's worse than Alcatraz, isn't it?
EILEEN/MONICA: See ya kid!
    (*Cut to:*)

EXT. STREET. NIGHT. MID-1950S. EILEEN'S WEDDING
Close-up of EILEEN *and* MONICA's *feet.*
Track (left to right) as their feet dance in time to EILEEN/MONICA's
voice over, singing 'R-A-G-M-M-O-P-P- RAGMOP!'
Cut to MONICA *and* EILEEN *in two-shot close-up.*
Track with them, right to left, as they dance back.
EILEEN/MONICA: (*Singing*) 'R-A-G-M-M-O-P-P- RAGMOP!'
    (*They laugh and collapse on to the doorstep.*
    Pan with them. Wedding celebration going on inside the house.
    They fan themselves with their hands.)
MONICA: God isn't it hot? I'm sweating past myself.
    (*Pause.*)
EILEEN: Here's Red Donnelly.
MONICA: Oh, that's all I need.
EILEEN: Arh, he's harmless.
    (*Cut to* EILEEN *and* MONICA's *point of view of Red*
    Donnelly.
    Pan with him as he walks to doorstep.
    He stops in front of them.)
RED: (*Winking at* MONICA) Hiya Mick!
    (*Cut to two-shot of* EILEEN *and* MONICA *on doorstep.*)
MONICA: (*Pointing her two forefingers at him*) Die!
    (RED *walks between them into the house.*)
RED: (*As he recedes into the house*) Oh what you're throwing
    away!
    (EILEEN *laughs.*)
MONICA: (*To* EILEEN) God help him – poor gobshite!
    (*Pause.*)
EILEEN: (*Laughing*) Remember Formby? And that tent?
MONICA: (*Embarrassed*) Oh God blimey!
    (*Cut to:*)

[94]

EXT. BEACH. DAY. EARLY 1950S

Mid three shot. A tent being erected.

EILEEN, *left of frame, holds centre pole.*

MONICA, *right of frame, is kneeling on the ground knocking pegs in with a mallet.*

JINGLES *is inside the tent itself.*

MONICA: I never.

JINGLES: (*Popping her head outside the tent flap*) You did.

MONICA: I never.

    (*Cut to close-up of* JINGLES.)

JINGLES: (*Adamant*) You did!

    (MONICA *rising into shot.*)

MONICA: (*Adamant*) I never!

JINGLES: You did fart!

    (*Puts her head back inside the tent.*

    A momentary pause.

    MONICA *hits* JINGLES *on the head with the mallet.*

    Slowly JINGLES' *form collapses accompanied by a low groan.*)

MONICA: (*Quietly*) I never.

    (*Cut to:*)

EXT. STREET. NIGHT. MID-1950S. EILEEN'S WEDDING

EILEEN: I thought you'd killed her, Micky.

MONICA: I know – so did I. When I think about it I was a real cow with that mallet, wasn't I?

    (*Pause.*)

    Do you ever see Jingles?

EILEEN: No – not since she married Les Shone.

    (*Pause.*

    Cut to mid shot of JINGLES.)

JINGLES: (*Throwing her arms wide and singing to the tune of Gershwin's "Swonderful"*) "Swonderful!'

    (*Cut to two shot of* EILEEN *and* MONICA *on doorstep.*)

EILEEN/MONICA: (*Singing*) "Smarvellous.'

    (*They get up and go to* JINGLES. *Pan with them to mid three shot. All hug one another.*)

EILEEN: Jingles! You came!

EILEEN: ⎫
MONICA: ⎬ (*Singing to the tune of 'Too Young'*) 'They tried to sell
JINGLES: ⎭   us Egg Foo Yung!'
    (*All laugh.*)
EILEEN: How are you doing, kid?
JINGLES: Smashing.
MONICA: Still married?
JINGLES: Oh God yeah! Two kids and a radiogram to support,
    know what I mean?
    (*Laughter. They walk towards the house. Pan with them.
    Dissolve to mid-long shot of the house. They go inside.*)
JINGLES: (*Voice over*) You haven't altered though, Ei – still not a
    pick on you.
EILEEN: (*Voice over*) Yeah – still eight stone soaking wet.
    (*Wedding guests come out on to the doorstep as the three disappear
    into the house.*)
JINGLES: (*Voice over*) How do you do it?
EILEEN: (*Voice over*) Witchcraft.
    (*Laughter.*)
JINGLES: (*Voice over*) You're looking well, Mick.
MONICA: (*Voice over*) Oh, but look at the size of me Jingles. I'm
    in a worse state than Russia.
JINGLES: (*Voice over*) Do you know who I saw in The Swan last
    week?
EILEEN: (*Voice over*) No. Who?
JINGLES: (*Voice over*) Jackie Mc-Gorrie.
EILEEN: (*Voice over*) Did you? Arh, remember the way we used to
    think that he was the dead spit of Burt Lancaster?
JINGLES: (*Voice over*) Yeah.
EILEEN: (*Voice over*) Arh, poor Jackie.
    (*Their voices fade.
    Cut to:*)

     INT. TRAIN COMPARTMENT. DAY. EARLY 1950S
Train travelling left to right.
Two shot of EILEEN *and* JINGLES *by the window.*
EILEEN, *left of frame, sitting opposite* JINGLES, *right of frame.*
Voice over of MONICA *singing 'Brr-Brr-Brr-Brr Busy Line'.*
They both turn and look at her and smile.

[96]

Cut to shot of MONICA *from* EILEEN *and* JINGLES' *point of view.*
She is half in the compartment, half in the corridor.
Cut to close-up of EILEEN. *She smiles but she is near to tears.*
She turns and looks out of the window.
Cut to:

INT. PARLOUR. DAY. EARLY 1950S

Close-up of EILEEN, *side view.*
EILEEN: (*Conciliatory*) Won't you say ta'ra, Dad?
  (*Silence.*)
  (*Hurt and angry*) I'm only going for the season.
  (*Cut to mid-long two shot.*
  EILEEN *in front of the sideboard, left of frame,* FATHER *by the
  fire, right of frame; he just leans forward and looks into the fire.*)
  (*Looking at him*) Do you know what? If I ever get a gun I'll
  blow your bleedin' brains out!

EXT. STREET. DAY. EARLY 1950S

Close-up of EILEEN *at taxi window.*
EILEEN: (*Putting a brave face on*) Ta'ra Mam!
  (*The cab moves off, left to right. Pan with it.*
  EILEEN *waves.*
  Cut to:)

INT. CAB. DAY. EARLY 1950S

Shot of MOTHER *from* EILEEN's *point of view from moving cab.*
MOTHER *on doorstep.*
MOTHER: (*Waves tearfully*) Bye, love – don't forget to write now,
  will you?
  (MOTHER, *still waving, recedes.*
  Cut to:)

INT. HOLIDAY-HOTEL DINING ROOM. MORNING.
EARLY 1950S

Mid long shot.
EILEEN, MONICA *and* JINGLES *in their black and white waitress
uniforms, at the head of their respective stations of tables. They are
very nervous.*
Silence.
Cut to their point of view of the tables which are now filled with

*musicians taking breakfast and all beating time with hands and cutlery
and singing 'R-A-G-M-O-P-P-P. RAGMOP!'*
EILEEN, MONICA, JINGLES *serving and clearing away.*
Musicians' voices fade.
MOTHER: (*Voice over*) Please come home Ei, your Dad's *really* ill.
  (*Cut to:*)

INT. HALLWAY. DAY. EARLY 1950S

Shot of street from front door. A taxi pulls up, right to left.
EILEEN *gets out.*
MOTHER: (*Voice over*) He thought it was ulcers right up till the end.
  (EILEEN *looks up at the house and then enters.*
  Cut to:)

INT. EILEEN/DAVE'S FLAT. NIGHT. LATE 1950S

Firelight.
Close shot, back view of EILEEN *as she looks into the fire.*
Silence. She turns her head to face the frame right.
DAVE: (*Voice over*) You're married now – I'm your husband – your
  duty's to me, frig everyone else. Monica, Jingles, that's all
  ancient history now.
  (*She turns to look back into the fire.*
  Cut to:)

INT. PARLOUR. NIGHT. EARLY 1950S. EILEEN'S WEDDING

Close-up of MONICA, *side view, at an upright piano.*
MONICA *sings 'Buttons and Bows'.*
GUEST: (*Voice over*) Go on Mick!
  (*She really begins to vamp it. She puts the piano lid down and gets
  up and sits on it.*
  EILEEN *and* JINGLES *stand at the back of the piano.*
  Cut to three shot of EILEEN, JINGLES *and* MONICA *singing.*
  Cut to:)

EXT. STREET. NIGHT. MID-1950S. EILEEN'S WEDDING

Close shot of doorstep.
EILEEN *on left of frame;* MAISIE, *right of frame and* TONY *sitting at a
right angle behind them. He is very drunk.*
Soundtrack of EILEEN, MONICA *and* JINGLES' *voices over singing*

the finale of 'Buttons and Bows'.
Applause and laughter, after a long pause.

MAISIE: Well, Ei – you're well and truly married now.

EILEEN: Yeah – but I don't feel *any* different, Maisie . . . I don't
feel any different.
(*Pause.*)

TONY: (*Drunk and sleepy, to no one in particular*) Don't be
worrying we'll be all right . . .
(*Dissolve to slightly wider shot of doorstep. People coming out.*
EILEEN, MAISIE, TONY *no longer on it. Wedding celebrations*
continue.
Soundtrack:)

MOTHER: (*Voice over*) They soon grow up . . . Maisie's engaged to
Georgie Roughley and I don't think it'll be long before our
Tony marries Rosie Forsyth . . .
(*Dissolve to slightly wider shot of house: front doorstep and*
parlour window. Front door closed. Window dark. Wedding
celebrations over.
All quiet.
Pause.
Soundtrack:)

MOTHER: (*Voice over*) I'll leave the place till morning . . .
(*Silence.*
Then crane slowly up diagonally over the front of the house until
the bedroom window is framed in darkness.
Track/zoom in on it.
Over the shot, soundtrack: the ending of Vaughan Williams'
Pastoral Symphony No. 3. The soprano singing a wordless song.
Song ends when bedroom window is framed.
Dissolve to:)

INT. BEDROOM. DAY

Track back very slowly from close-up of window.
A bright sunshine. Curtains billowing. Silence.

MOTHER: (*Voice over*) I love the light nights . . .

MAISIE: (*As an adult, voice over*) But they're starting to draw in
now, aren't they, Mam?

MOTHER: (*Voice over*) Yeah.
(*Pause.*

[99]

Distant rolling thunder.
Pause.)
FATHER: (*Voice over*) Nellie . . . Nellie! . . . Nell! . . .
    (*His voice fades.*
    Thunder rolling vaguely in the background.
    Dissolve.)

INT. KITCHEN. EARLY SUMMER EVENING
Panning shot to mirror on sideboard, make-up strewn in front of it.
When mirror is framed hold.
Soundtrack:
EILEEN: (*As adult, voice over*) Sorry about the mess, Mam . . .
MOTHER: (*Voice over*) Go on – you're all right – I'll see to it . . .
EILEEN: Thanks Mam . . .
MONICA: } (*Voice over*) See yer Mrs D. . . .
JINGLES: Ta'ra . . .
    (*The sound of them going out.*)
MOTHER: (*Voice over, calling after them*) Enjoy yourselves!
    (*Pan away from mirror.*
    Dissolve to panning shot of ironing board. Pan stops when ironing
    board is framed.
    MOTHER *is sprinkling water from a cup on to handkerchiefs, then*
    – after ironing them with a flat iron – she folds them and puts them
    into a pile on the end of the ironing board.
    Dissolve to close-up of MOTHER *at ironing board.*
    She picks up a flat iron, holds it close to her cheek, to test it for heat,
    spits on it, then continues ironing.
    Soundtrack:)
TONY: (*Voice over, as adult*) Goodnight, Mahsie.
MOTHER: (*Voice over*) Goodnight, son.
    (*Dissolve:*)

INT. PARLOUR. NIGHT
Parlour in firelight.
Mid-wide shot of MOTHER *sitting in a chair, reading newspaper.*
EILEEN, MAISIE, TONY, *as children, sitting around her on the floor.*
They are ready for bed and drinking their cocoa.
Silence.
MAISIE: (*As a child, quietly*) Look, Mam – my cocoa's got half a

crown on it . . .
(MOTHER *looks up and smiles. Children continue drinking.*
MOTHER *stares into the fire and sighs.*
Silence.
Dissolve to panning shot across parlour.
Newspaper on chair, toys strewn across the mat in front of the hearth.
Firelight.
Soundtrack:)
MOTHER: (*Voice over*) Come on – up the dancers!
(*Children giggling as they go upstairs.*)
How much do you love me?
CHILDREN: A pound of sugar!
(*Laughter.*
Their voices fade.
Pause.)
MOTHER: (*Voice over, singing with a rocking motion*) Hush-a-
bowee . . .
  Hush-a-bow . . .
(*Her voice fades.*
Dissolve to MOTHER *in parlour in firelight.*
Track in on her.
She is sleeping in the chair, her head on her chest, her mouth open. The newspaper slips to the floor.
Soundtrack:)
(*Voice over*) The Sandman is coming . . .
(*Dissolve to shot of* MOTHER *sitting in armchair in bright sunshine.*
She is bathed in and surrounded by light. Slowly she looks up and smiles.
Dissolve to firelight.
Pan to fire.
Track in on fire.
Soundtrack:)
(*Voice over*) How much do you love me?
(*Continue tracking in on fire.*
Fade to black.
Closing credits.)

[101]

Still Lives

NB:
Still Lives continues the story of *Distant Voices* and takes place in
Liverpool in the closing years of the 1950s.

It begins with a birth and ends with a marriage – these two
great rituals forming the parameters within which the family's
subtle but gradual disintegration takes place.

As in painting, the drama lies not so much in the bowl of fruit
or the vase of flowers but the ways in which these objects are
perceived – in effect, stasis as drama.

All the family history is packed into *Distant Voices*, while in
Still Lives life has reached an even keel and ticks silently away.

Liverpool 1955–1959

Blackness.
Fade up on main title, Still Lives.
Fade out main title.
Fade up on:

EXT. NIGHT

Close-up of water. River Mersey, dark and rippling. Rain.
Track and pan.
Soundtrack: a choir singing unaccompanied Britten's 'A Hymn To
The Virgin':

    'Of one that is so fair and bright,
    Velut maris stella,
    Brighter than the day is light,
    Parens et puella:
    I cry to thee, thou see to me,
    Lady, pray thy son for me,
    Tam pia.
    That I may come to thee
    Maria . . .'

(Dissolve to:)

INT. HOSPITAL LABOUR WARD. NIGHT

Close-up of hands grasping the bed-rail, side view.
Screaming is heard.
Hold.
Soundtrack: 'A Hymn To The Virgin' continued:

    'All this world was forlorn
    Eva peccatrice,
    Till our lord was y-born,
    De te genetrice . . .'

Track down the bed to close-up of MAISIE *(side view).*
She is in dry labour.
MAISIE: *(Screaming)* Oh God! God!

    (Soundtrack: 'A Hymn To The Virgin' continued.
      'With ave it went away

[105]

Darkest night, and comes the day,
Salutis,
The well springeth out of thee,
Virtutis . . .'
(*Dissolve to:*)

INT. HOSPITAL. NIGHT
A newly born baby girl naked and screaming being handed from one
pair of gloved hands to another, against blackness.
Dissolve to:

INT. CHURCH. SUNDAY. LATE MORNING
The baby in its christening robes being handed to PRIEST'*s hands.*
Dissolve to baby in PRIEST'*s arms.*
PRIEST: (*Voice over*) I baptize thee Elaine . . .
(*Pours water on baby's head. Baby cries.*)
In the name of the Father, and of the Son, and of the Holy
Ghost . . .
(*Dissolve to close shot of* MAISIE *and her husband* GEORGE *at*
the font.
The PRIEST *finishes baptizing the baby and hands her to*
MAISIE. MAISIE *cradles her.*
Slowly track back.
Soundtrack: 'A Hymn To The Virgin' continued:
'Lady, flower of everything,
Rosa sine spina,
Thou bare jesu, heaven's king
Gratia divina . . .'
Track stops when MAISIE, GEORGE, PRIEST *and entire family*
are seen in tableau at the font.
Soundtrack: 'A Hymn To The Virgin' continued:
'Of all thou barest the prize
Lady, queen of Paradise,
Electa,
Maid mild, mother es effecta.'
Baby wailing. People smiling.
Dissolve to:)

[106]

EXT. STREET. SUNDAY. MIDDAY

MOTHER's *house seen in mid-long shot. Bright sunshine.* MAISIE's *pram outside the front door. Front door open. Parlour window open. Curtains billowing.*
Soundtrack: 'Family Favourites' theme-tune is heard ('With A Song in My Heart').

BBC ANNOUNCER: This is Family Favourites introduced by Jean Metcalfe and Bill –
 (*Fade* ANNOUNCER's *voice.*
 Soundmix to Dicky Valentine singing 'The Finger of Suspicion'.
 MAISIE *comes out of the house, takes the child from the pram, then goes back inside.*
 Soundtrack of Dicky Valentine singing continues.
 Dissolve to:)

INT. MUM'S HOUSE. EARLY AFTERNOON. SUNDAY

Parlour. Close-up of GEORGE *asleep in the armchair, side view. Soundtrack:*

BILLY COTTON: (*Voice over*) Wakey! Way-kee!
 (*Signature tune of 'The Billy Cotton Band Show'.*)

BBC ANNOUNCER: It's the Billy Cotton Band Show starring . . .
 (*Soundmix: fade to music being played by Billy Cotton Band then cross-fade to voice over from show:*)
 Hey you! You down there with the glasses! Don't I know you?
 (*Laughter.*
 Dissolve to close-up of TONY, *side view, listening to 'Beyond Our Ken' on radio.*
 Soundtrack: soundmix to a 'Rodney and Charles' sketch or 'That was an excerpt from' at the show's opening.
 Laughter.
 TONY *laughing.*
 Applause. Laughter.
 Soundtrack:)

BBC ANNOUNCER: You might have been listening to or have just missed 'Beyond Our Ken' – a sort of radio show in which you heard Kenneth Horne, Kenneth Williams, Hugh Paddick, Betty Marsden and Bill Pertwee. The script, believe it or not, was written . . .

(*Fade sound.*
Dissolve to:)

EXT. MOTHER'S HOUSE. SUNDAY AFTERNOON

MOTHER *is seen in medium close-up at the parlour window, from the*
street. Bright sunshine.
The window is half open and she is sitting inside the parlour with her
left arm lying along the outside of the windowsill. Her arm is the only
part of her clearly seen – the rest of her face and body is behind the
heavy net curtain.
She looks out into the street.
MOTHER: (*Voice over*) Will you make us a lemon dash, Tony?
  (*Dissolve to:*)

INT. PARLOUR. SUNDAY AFTERNOON

Mid shot of MAISIE *cradling the baby, side view.*
MAISIE *is singing 'The Birthday of the Little Princess' softly to the*
child. The child is asleep. She puts her in the cot.
Soundtrack:
Soundmix to EILEEN's *voice over singing 'Brown-skinned Girl'.*
Cut to:

INT. PUB PARLOUR. CHRISTENING CELEBRATIONS. NIGHT

EILEEN *and* DAVE *in medium close-up.*
EILEEN *sings 'Brown-skinned Girl'.*
The guests begin to join in except DAVE *who drinks silently.*
Pan around right to left on singing guests. Pan ends when MAISIE *and*
MOTHER *are in medium close-up. All finish the song in chorus.*
Laughter. Applause. Smiles.
Jib or crane up and track forward to the narrow passage leading from
the parlour to the bar. It is crowded.
GEORGE *in medium close-up, ordering drinks.*
Soundtrack:
GUEST: (*Voice over, singing*) 'Oh my! What a rotten song,
    What a rotten song,
    What a rotten song,
    Oh my! What a rotten song,
    What a rotten singer too!'
  (*Laughter. Applause.*)

[108]

GEORGE: Can I have – a rum and pep, a rum and blackcurrant, a black and tan, half a shandy, a pint of bitter, a pint of mild, a mild and bitter mixed . . .

(TONY – *preceded by his girlfriend* ROSE – *enters and they both walk towards the camera.*)

(*To* ROSE) Hi yer Rose – come to wet the baby's head?

ROSE: Oh, I wouldn't miss it for the world.

TONY: (*To* GEORGE) Well – how does it feel to be a dad?

GEORGE: Oh – made up!

(TONY *and* ROSE *walk into the parlour.*)

(*Calling after them*) What are you having?

(*Cut to medium close-up, two shot.* MAISIE *and* MOTHER.)

MOTHER: ⎱ Hello Rose
MAISIE: ⎰ Hello son
(*Together*) ⎰ OK Tone?

(*Cut to medium close-up. Two shot.* TONY *and* ROSE.)

TONY: Hi yer Maise.

How's Maisie eh?

ROSE: How are you, Mrs D?

Hello Maisie.

MAISIE: (*Voice over*) Smashing!

MOTHER: (*Voice over*) Still working at the English Electric, Rose?

ROSE: Oh God yer! I'm there for life I think.

DAVE: (*Voice over*) All right Tone?

EILEEN: (*Voice over*) Hi yer – Rose!

(ROSE *looks in their direction.*)

ROSE: Hello Ei, Dave.

(*Cut to medium close-up. Two shot.* EILEEN *and* DAVE.)

DAVE: Hello girl.

EILEEN: How are you, Tone?

(*Cut to medium close-up. Two shot.* TONY *and* ROSE. TONY *gives thumbs up sign.*)

(*Cut to medium close-up of a pint glass on the table, which is covered with drinks.*)

TONY: (*Voice over*) Let's have a kitty, eh? A pound a man?

(*Pound notes being put into the pint glass and thrown on to the table.*)

(*Cut to medium close-up. Two shot.* MAISIE *and* MOTHER. MOTHER *right of frame, full-faced.* MAISIE *in profile left of frame.*

MOTHER *begins to sing 'When That Old Gang of Mine' and everyone begins to join in.*
Pan slowly round guests left to right, as they sing along.
Fade singing and all sync sound, but guests continue to sing as we continue to pan.
Soundtrack:)
MR HYAMS: *(Voice over, calling)* Rent!
TONY: *(Voice over, calling)* Spent!
   (Fade to white.
   Soundtrack as we hold on white.)
MOTHER: *(Voice over)* Oh don't, Tony – he'll think you're
   serious. *(Calling)* Come in Mr Hyams – the money's on the
   sideboard.
   (Fade from white to:)

EXT. STREET. OUTSIDE MOTHER'S HOUSE.
EARLY FRIDAY EVENING. SUMMER
It is light. MR SPAULL, *the insurance man, riding a bike around the corner and stopping at* MOTHER's *front door. When riding the bike he is free-wheeling – standing on one pedal on one side of the bike. Pan with him to the front door, right to left.*
He props his bike up against the low wall in front of the house and goes to the front door.
Cut to:

INT. HALL. MOTHER'S HOUSE. EARLY FRIDAY EVENING.
SUMMER
Looking down the hall towards the street.
MR SPAULL *comes to the door.*
MR SPAULL: *(Calling down the hall)* Royal Liver!
MOTHER: *(From the parlour, voice over)* Come in, Mr Spaull.
   (He comes down the hall and goes into the parlour.)
   (Cut to:)

INT. PARLOUR. MUM'S HOUSE. EARLY FRIDAY EVENING.
SUMMER
Close-up of MOTHER.
MOTHER: Can I surrender the policies on the two girls, Mr
   Spaull?

[110]

(*Cut to mid shot* (*head-on*) *of* MR SPAULL. *He is sitting on a chair near the door, next to the sideboard, which is on his left.*)

MR SPAULL: (*As he marks the books*) Certainly, Mrs Davies. (*Looking at the policies*) You've had these some time now, haven't you?

(*Cut to close-up of* MOTHER.)

MOTHER: Yer – I've had them since they were babies. I started paying them when it was only a penny a week – but as they're both married now there's no point in keeping them on. They've got their own insurance now.

MR SPAULL: (*Voice over*) All right, Mrs Davies, I'll take them into the office for you.

MOTHER: Thanks, Mr Spaull. See you next week.

(*Cut to medium close-up of* MR SPAULL *from* MOTHER'*s point of view.*)

MR SPAULL: (*Getting up and leaving*) Ta-ta.

(*Cut to medium close-up of sideboard. On it, rent book, insurance books, club book with money on it.*)

MOTHER: (*Voice over*) Tony!

TONY: (*Voice over*) Yer?

(*Fade to white.*)

MOTHER: (*Voice over*) I'm just running to Confession. Will you pay the clubman for me if he comes?

TONY: (*Voice over*) OK Mam.

(*Fade from white to:*)

INT. PUB PARLOUR. CHRISTENING CELEBRATIONS. NIGHT

Panning slowly around guests right to left. They are singing but no sync sound is heard.

Soundtrack:

MOTHER: (*Voice over*) I borrow £25 from the Leigh and Lend every Christmas then pay it back over the next twelve months – it's like a tontine really . . .

(*Fade up singing. Continue panning, as they sing. Pan stops on* MAISIE *and* MARGIE *in medium close-up two shot. Singing finishes. Applause. Laughter.*)

MARGIE: And how much did she weigh?

MAISIE: Just over seven pounds.

MARGIE: She was a big baby wasn't she?

[111]

MAISIE: Yeah.

MARGIE: Did you have her at Mill Road?

MAISIE: Yer – on the 6th.

MARGIE: What have you called her?

MAISIE: Elaine.

MARGIE: Arh – God love her! (*To* MOTHER) And how d'you like being a gran, Mrs D?
    (*Cut to close-up of* MOTHER.)

MOTHER: Oh I wouldn't be without her – well she's my first – she's lovely.
    (*Cut to medium close-up two shot.* MARGIE *and* MAISIE.)

MARGIE: Well Maise – I'd better be making tracks.

MAISIE: Thanks for coming, Margie. I'll see ya.

MARGIE: (*Getting up*) See you Maisie.
    Ta'ra Mrs D. (*Exits.*)
    (*Pan to medium close-up two shot.* MUM *and* MAISIE.)

MOTHER: (*To Margie*) Ta'ra love. (*To* MAISIE) You've known Margie for some years, haven't you, Maise?

MAISIE: Yer – we've all been mates since school . . .
    (*Fade to white.*)

MAISIE: (*Voice over*) Margie, myself and Vera Large . . .

MOTHER: (*Voice over*) Vera's a nice girl, isn't she?

MAISIE: (*Voice over*) Arh smashing.

MOTHER: (*Voice over*) Is *she* still working?
    (*Fade from white.*)

MAISIE: Yeah – she's still at Paton Calverts.

INT. HALL. MOTHER'S HOUSE. EARLY SATURDAY EVENING.
SUMMER

It is light.

Medium close-up DOREEN MATHER's *face at the front door. She is mentally retarded and constantly pushes her tongue in and out of her mouth between pursed lips. She knocks on the front door. No answer. She just stands there.*

Pause.

Silence.

DOREEN *sings from* 'Dreamboat' *softly to herself.*

DOREEN: (*Calling down hall*) Maisie!
    (*Cut to mid shot of empty hall from* DOREEN's *point of view.*

Silence.
Cut to mid-long shot of DOREEN *from bottom of stairs.*
Pause.
She just stands there, looking down the hall.
Then slowly she begins to turn a circle on the doorstep, singing
softly to herself as she does so.
She stops singing. Silence. She just stands there.)
MAISIE: (*Voice over*) Have you come to mind the baby Doreen?
DOREEN: Yeah.
MAISIE: (*Voice over*) Come in then, love.
    (*Slowly, clumsily,* DOREEN *walks down the hall towards the*
    camera. Fade to white.)
MAISIE: (*Voice over*) . . . and Louis . . . she went to live on that
    new estate they've just built in Kirkby . . .
    (*Fade from white.*)

INT. PUB PARLOUR. CHRISTENING CELEBRATIONS. NIGHT
Medium close-up, two shot. MAISIE *and* MOTHER.
MAISIE: (*To* MOTHER) . . . you remember little Louis – she lived
    in Keble Street . . . she always used to sing 'Deep Purple'.
MOTHER: Oh I know! Yer!
MONICA: (*Voice over*) Maisie Davies – you dirty mare!
MAISIE: (*Laughing*) Hi yer – Micky!
MONICA: (*Voice over*) Hi yer Mrs D!
MOTHER: (*Laughing*) You're looking well, Mick.
    (*Cut to medium close-up, two shot.* MONICA *and her husband,*
    RED.)
MONICA: I know – the face that launched a thousand ships.
RED: The other way.
MONICA: That's wicked that – being married to you no wonder
    my poor face is destroyed. If I'd played my cards right I'd be
    in America now. (*To* MAISIE *and* MOTHER) Remember that
    yank I went out with, Mrs D? He thought I had lovely
    eyes . . .
MONICA/RED: . . . hated the rest of me but thought I had lovely
    eyes!
    (*Laughter*)
    And I end up by falling for a dwarf. There's no justice you
    know, is there?

(*Cut to two shot. Medium close-up.* MAISIE *and* MOTHER. *They laugh.*

Cut to two shot. Medium close-up. MONICA *and* RED. *He puts his arms around her waist from behind and cuddles her.*)

RED: (*Singing*) 'Chocolate eyes! Those great big chocolate eyes!'

MONICA: Get your hands off my body.

RED: (*Still cuddling her*) Arh – you've only got one tonsil but I love you all the same!

MONICA: Don't make mock of Mick! (*Aside*) Bastard!

(*Cut to medium close-up of* MAISIE.)

MAISIE: Now – you know you love the bones of him really.

(*Cut to two shot. Medium close-up.* MONICA *and* RED.)

MONICA: Yer – I married him 'cos he's dead sensitive. Dead from the neck up – sensitive from the waist down.

(RED *cuddles her from behind even more.*)

RED: O O O H H H!

MONICA: (*To* MAISIE *and* MOTHER, *indicating* RED) The walking hormone. (*To* RED – *laughing*) Oh you fool!

(*Walks off. Camera left.*

RED *sits down next to* MAISIE.

Pan down with him.)

RED: (*Clapping his hands together and looking at* TONY) Pound a man, is it?

(*Cut to medium close-up, two shot.* EILEEN *and* DAVE.)

DAVE: (*Getting up and exiting frame*) 'E' are – Mick – sit here.

MONICA: (*Entering frame and sitting down beside* EILEEN) Thanks Dave.

DAVE: (*Voice over*) (*Calling to* RED) Go the match yesterday Red?

EILEEN: Oh eh Dave – you're not talking about football again, are you?

(*Cut to close-up.* DAVE *from* EILEEN's *point of view. Back view.*)

DAVE: (*Looking back over his shoulder as he walks to* RED) Oh behave, will you!

(DAVE *walks towards* RED.

Cut to two shot. Medium close-up. EILEEN *and* MONICA.)

EILEEN: Football mad.

MONICA: Aren't they all? Look at the thing I'm married to. He gets more worked up over a set of fixtures than me in my

[114]

nude – d'you know what? If I was a centre forward I'd be
laughing.

(*Cut to medium close-up of* RED, *already standing.*)

RED: (*Calling to* MONICA) What are you having, blossom?

(DAVE *enters shot.*

Cut to two shot. Medium close-up of EILEEN *and* MONICA.)

MONICA: A rum and pep, love.

EILEEN: (*to* RED) And then *you*!

MONICA: He should be so lucky!

EILEEN: (*To* DAVE) Eh Dave will you get us some ciggies?

DAVE: (*Voice over*) Craven A?

EILEEN: Or Park Drive.

(*Cut to two shot. Medium close-up.* RED *and* DAVE.)

DAVE: (*To* EILEEN) OK. (*To* RED) What's your poison, Red?

(*They walk to the bar in the passage.*

Track or pan with them.)

RED: A brown over bitter thanks, Dave.

(*Cut to medium close-up, two shot.* TONY *and* ROSE.

TONY *starts singing* 'I Want a Girl'. *Everyone begins to join in.*

Fade sound although TONY *and* ROSE *and all continue to sing.*

Hold.

Fade to white.)

MOTHER: (*Voice over*) You're home early lad. Come on in.

TONY: (*Voice over*) Oh but you've only just done the lobby mam.

MOTHER: (*Voice over*) No – go on – you're all right.

(TONY's *footsteps are heard along the hall.*

Fade from white.)

INT. HALL. MOTHER'S HOUSE. EARLY FRIDAY EVENING.
SUMMER

It is light.

Low-angled medium close-up of MOTHER *looking out towards the
street. She is kneeling and scrubbing the last part of the hall floor by
the front door.*

MOTHER: (*Looking up*) Your tea's in the oven, son.

TONY: (*Voice over*) OK Mam.

(*She continues scrubbing.*

Hold.

Cut to close-up of TONY *at the end of the hall by the kitchen door.*

*He is wearing only pants and a singlet and has just finished
washing. He is drying his face with a towel. He stands for a
moment just looking at* MOTHER.)

TONY: Are you going to come and have yours, Mam?

MOTHER: (*Voice over*) I'll be in in a minute, lad.

(TONY *continues looking at her. His eyes fill with tears.*)

TONY: OK Mam.

(*Hold on* TONY.

Fade to white.)

MOTHER: (*Voice over*) Your shirt is ironed, son – it's on the rack
with the hankies.

TONY: (*Voice over*) Thanks, Mahsie.

(*Fade from white.*)

INT. PUB PARLOUR. CHRISTENING CELEBRATIONS. NIGHT

Medium close-up, two shot. TONY *and* ROSE. *Everyone is singing
though no sound can be heard. Gradually fade up sound of* TONY
and all singing 'I Want A Girl'.

Cut to medium close-up, two shot. MAISIE *and* GEORGE.

MAISIE *starts singing* 'Mississippi Honeymoon', *which first*
GEORGE, *then the others, join in.*

Pan around left to right. All singing.

Pan ends on medium close-up of MONICA *and* EILEEN.

EXT. PUB CHRISTENING CELEBRATIONS. NIGHT

Two shots of JINGLES *and* LES, *head on.*

JINGLES: (*Coaxing*) Come on, Les, just one drink.

(*Soundtrack of all singing* 'Mississippi Honeymoon' *inside the
pub.*)

LES: (*Bellicose*) All right, just one drink, just to wet the baby's
head, but I'm not staying here all fucking night!

JINGLES: OK, Les, OK.

(*They enter the pub –* LES *first,* JINGLES *after.*

Cut to:)

INT. PUB CHRISTENING CELEBRATIONS. NIGHT

Mid-long shot. LES *and* JINGLES *walk into the passage which leads
from the parlour to the bar.* LES *stands at the bar with* TONY,
GEORGE, DAVE *and* RED. JINGLES *continues towards camera and*

[116]

exits into the parlour.
Soundtrack:
EILEEN: (*Voice over*) What's the matter with Pontius?
JINGLES: (*Voice over*) Oh, yer know, the usual.
MONICA: (*Voice over*) Look at the face on that – stop a bleeding
    clock!
    (LES *is laughing and joking with the other men.*)
TONY: (*To* LES) Are you having a bevy or what?
    (*Hold on group in passage.*)
ALL: (*Singing*) 'We're all together again
      So here we are.
      We're all together again
      So here we are . . .'
    (*Cut to mid-long shot.*
    JINGLES, *back to camera, sitting on a stool facing* EILEEN *and*
    MONICA.)
ALL: (*Singing*) 'And the lord knows when
      We'll be together again
      So we're all together again
      So here we are.'
    (EILEEN *and* MONICA *start to sing* 'Back in the Old Routine'.
    Everyone joins in but it is the three girls' special song.
    Track in on the three girls very slowly as they sing.
    Track continues in and around on JINGLES. *Track stops when*
    she is in mid-shot, side view.
    Throughout the song she has been getting more and more upset.
    When the last verse is reached she breaks down completely.
    EILEEN *and* MONICA *kneel into shot by* JINGLES' *stool.*)
EILEEN: Oh, Jingles, don't get so upset.
MONICA: Arh – come on.
JINGLES: (*Bringing herself under control*) No – I'm all right –
    honest. It's just Les – you know what he's like when he
    turns.
EILEEN: The bastard! For two pins I'd go over there and tell him!
JINGLES: No – don't say anything, Ei.
MONICA: They're all the same – when they're not using the big
    stick, they're farting – aren't men horrible?
    (*Cut to:*)

INT. PUB. PASSAGE LEADING TO THE PARLOUR.
CHRISTENING CELEBRATIONS. NIGHT

Mid shot. LES *in the passage on his own.*

LES: (*Looking at* JINGLES *and motioning her to come*) Eh! Come
on!
(*Cut to:*)

INT. PUB PARLOUR. CHRISTENING CELEBRATIONS . NIGHT

Medium close-up of JINGLES, *side view.*

JINGLES *quickly looks around at* LES *and quickly finishes her drink.*

EILEEN: (*Voice over*) Oh you're not going are you Jingles?

JINGLES: I think Les wants to.
(*She looks anxiously around.*)

MONICA: (*Voice over*) But you've only been here five minutes.
(*Cut to:*)

INT. PUB. PASSAGE LEADING TO THE PARLOUR.
CHRISTENING CELEBRATIONS. NIGHT

Close-up of LES *in passage.*

LES: (*Even more belligerent*) Come on!
(*Cut to:*)

INT. PUB PARLOUR. CHRISTENING CELEBRATIONS. NIGHT

Close-up of EILEEN *and* MONICA.

EILEEN: I feel like going over there and bursting him!
(*Cut to medium close-up of* JINGLES *from* MONICA *and*
EILEEN's *point of view.* LES *is in the background walking out.*)

JINGLES: (*Getting up*) I'd better go Ei. See ya, Micky.
(JINGLES *walks away, very upset.*
Cut to two shot, medium close-up. MAISIE *and* MOTHER. *They
watch her go.*)

MOTHER: I wonder what's wrong.

MAISIE: I think Jingles is having a bad time with Les.

MOTHER: It's not right, you know.
(*Cut to mid-wide shot of* JINGLES.
She walks out behind a seated TONY.
Possibly pan with her.)

TONY: (*Sympathetic*) Never mind, girl.

JINGLES (*Breaking down again*) See yer, Tone.

(JINGLES *exits*.
Cut to mid three shot of EILEEN, *centre frame,* DAVE, *left of frame,* MONICA, *right of frame*.)

EILEEN: Poor Jingles.

DAVE: You sit there! It's none of your business. Don't get involved.

(*Cut to close-up of* EILEEN.)

EILEEN: You callous bleeder! That's my friend that. You men – you're all the bleeding same – you only think of yourselves.

(*Cut to close-up of* DAVE.)

DAVE: Don't you tell me what I think. No one knows what's going on inside my mind.

(*Cut to close-up of* EILEEN.)

EILEEN: Including you.

(*Cut to close-up of* DAVE.)

DAVE: You can't argue with you – women are different from men.

(*Cut to two shot, medium close-up of* EILEEN *and* MONICA.)

EILEEN: Oh, so you've noticed? (*To* MONICA) Isn't he quick?

(*Cut to two shot. Medium close-up of* DAVE *and* TONY.)

TONY: (*To* EILEEN) Heck! Heck! What's going on?

EILEEN: (*Voice over, angry*) Nothing!

TONY: All right, don't bite my head off.

DAVE: You know the way she flies off the handle for the least thing.

(*Cut to close-up of* EILEEN *and* MONICA.)

EILEEN: (*Now very angry*) I don't! I've got good cause to! You closet!

(*Cut to two shot. Medium close-up of* MOTHER *and* MAISIE *from* EILEEN'*s point of view*.)

MOTHER: (*To* EILEEN) Now – come on! We don't want any upset.

EILEEN: (*Voice over*) OK Mam.

DAVE: (*Voice over*) OK Nell.

MOTHER: We're here to enjoy ourselves. Come on Micky – give us a song.

(*Cut to two shot. Medium close-up of* MONICA *and* EILEEN *from* MOTHER'*s point of view*. MONICA *tries to diffuse the situation by singing* 'Bye Bye Blackbird'.
Cut to close-up of RED.)

[119]

RED: (*Good-naturedly*) Oh God blimey – you're not singing again are you, Mick?

(*Cut to close-up of* MONICA.)

MONICA: (*Equally good-natured*) Listen, bloated tonsils – just because you're dead miserable doesn't mean to say that the rest of us have got to go round looking like 'keep death off the road'.

(*All sing* 'Bye Bye Blackbird'.

Cut to close-up of RED.)

RED: Judy Garland in bad health.

(*Cut to two shot. Medium close-up of* EILEEN *and* MONICA.)

MONICA: Oh my arse!

(*She joins in the singing and encourages* EILEEN *to do so.* EILEEN *responds reluctantly.*

Then EILEEN *starts singing* '*I Want To Be Around*'.)

MONICA: Go on Ei! I love this song.

(*Pan to* EILEEN *in close-up, singing solo. Applause when she finishes song.*)

MONICA: (*Voice over*) Oh it's a smashing song, that.

(*Cut to the passage leading to the parlour.* TONY *in mid shot at the bar, side view, waiting to order drinks.*

Soundtrack: Guests in parlour singing '*I Loved the Ladies*'.)

TONY: (*To barmaid*) Two halves of shandy. A mackies. A Double Diamond. A pale ale and lime. A Black and Tan. Mild over bitter. A rum and Pep. A rum and blackcurrant. And a Guinness.

(*He stands at the bar getting the money ready. He acknowledges friends and neighbours as they pass him by while he waits for the drinks.*)

Hello Moggie.

Hiyer Ritchie (etc.).

(*Soundtrack: Guests in parlour, singing.*

The barmaid hands the drinks on a tray over the heads of the people at the bar. TONY *takes them and pays her.*)

Thanks Nora, and have one for yourself.

NORA: Thanks Tony.

(*Soundtrack: Guests in parlour singing* '*I Love the Ladies*'.

TONY *turns and walks towards the parlour.*

Cut to medium close-up of TONY *and* ROSE. *They all continue to sing.*

Cut to medium close-up, three shot of GEORGE, MAISIE *and* MOTHER.
Cut to medium close-up, two shot of DAVE *and* RED. *The song continues.*
Cut to two shot, medium close-up of MONICA *and* EILEEN. *Laughter. Applause.*)

RED: (*Voice over*) Come on Mick.

MONICA: OK. In a minute. I'll just finish my drink.

IVY: (*Voice over*) Come on! Let's have your glasses please!
(EILEEN *and* MONICA *drink up.*)
Cut to medium close-up of RED.

RED: Oh hey Mick – come on!
(*Cut to two shot, medium close-up of* EILEEN *and* MONICA *still trying to finish their drinks.*)

MONICA: Ignore him.
(*Cut to wide shot, looking towards the door leading to the street.* TONY, GEORGE *and* DAVE *walk out, followed by* RED. *As he goes to the parlour door he turns to* MONICA.)

RED: Come on Keemosabbie!
(*Cut to two shot. Medium close-up of* EILEEN *and* MONICA.)

MONICA: All right Tonto! Oh men – don't they mither? (*She puts down her still unfinished drink.*) I'd better go, otherwise he'll get a cobb on.

EILEEN: You're not frightened of him are you?

MONICA: Am I shite! He looks at me the wrong way I give him a dog's life.
(*They get up and leave.*
Cut to wide shot, looking towards the door which leads towards the street.
MONICA *and* EILEEN *enter the frame and walk towards the door.*)

EILEEN: Is he still handy around the house?

MONICA: You're joking aren't you? That thing won't do a tap. He changed a nappy once – nearly had a nervous breakdown.
(*As they exit, they are followed by a few people. Those remaining in the parlour begin to sing 'The Road to Anywhere'.*
Cut to:)

[121]

EXT. PUB. CHRISTENING CELEBRATIONS. NIGHT
Wide shot, head on, of TONY, GEORGE, DAVE *and* RED *in a heated but friendly discussion about football – the 1958/59 season.*
Soundtrack vaguely in the background of people in parlour singing inside the pub. Some people come out followed by EILEEN *and* MONICA, *who stand talking.*

IVY: (*Voice over, from inside the pub*) Come on now! Can I have your glasses – *PLEASE!*
(*Cut to two shot. Medium close-up, head on.* EILEEN, *left of frame profile,* MONICA, *centre frame full face.*
Soundtrack of people singing inside the pub.)

MONICA: (*To* RED) Red . . . Red! (*To* EILEEN) See what I mean? Doesn't take a blind bit of notice. It's like talking to a corpse. (*To* RED) Hey, soft shite! You said you wanted to go before.
(*Cut to mid shot of group of* TONY, GEORGE, DAVE *and* RED, *side view,* MONICA's *point of view.*)

RED: God blimey! It's worse than the SS this! I can have a talk can't I?
(*Continues talking to the others.*
Cut to two shot, medium close-up, head on of EILEEN *and* MONICA.)

MONICA: Oh God help us – it's alive!

EILEEN: Men!

MONICA: (*American accent*) The little dears! (*To* EILEEN) So don't be a stranger – otherwise I'll not see you till next Preston Guild. We're only in Jubilee Drive – you're only ten minutes away.

EILEEN: (*Half-hearted*) We'll see . . . I'll try and come round.

MONICA: Or I could come over to yours. You're only in Vane Street aren't you?

EILEEN: Oh you'd better not, Micky, he's funny about having visitors.

MONICA: (*A bit hurt at being put off*) OK. Then you try and come to me.

EILEEN: (*Still half-hearted*) We'll see, kid.
(*An awkward silence between them.*)

MONICA: Well, I'd better get Father Feck home.
(*She walks to* RED. *Pan with her.*)

(*To* RED) Come on Trigger – back to the reservation.
(*She takes him by the arm and they walk up the street.*
Goodnights all round. MONICA *waves to* EILEEN *but without*
turning to her.
Continue panning with MONICA.
Cut to mid-shot of EILEEN, *full face. She watches* MONICA *and*
RED *go. Her eyes fill with tears.*
Through the pub door behind EILEEN, MOTHER, MAISIE,
ROSE *and other guests come streaming out into the street, singing*
'*I Will If You Will So Will I*'.)

MAISIE: (*Linking* EILEEN'*s arm*) Come on Ei!
(EILEEN *turns and walks down the street with* MAISIE *and the*
others.
TONY, GEORGE *and* DAVE *follow. All sing* '*Singing I Will If*
You Will'.)

GUEST: Hitchiecoo!
(*They all go down the street. Their voices drift away.*
Cut to:)

EXT. ALLEY LEADING TO GRAN'S HOUSE.
CHRISTENING CELEBRATIONS. NIGHT

DAVE *and* EILEEN *in medium close-up, back view, walking towards*
the house. DAVE *drunk.*
Soundtrack of MAISIE'*s voice singing* '*Barney Google*'.
Track with EILEEN *and* DAVE.

DAVE: (*Very loud, very drunk*) I've had a ball!

EILEEN: (*An intense whisper*) Do you have to shout? You'll wake
the dead.

GRAN: (*Voice over, angry, from inside the house*) Is that you Eileen?

EILEEN: Oh God blimey you have!
(EILEEN *and* DAVE *stop walking.*
Track stops.)
(*Placatory*) Yer – it's only me and Dave Gran . . . we'll be in
in a minute.

DAVE: I wanna wee.

EILEEN: Oh then do it over there – and be quick.
(DAVE *goes to the wall, exiting camera left.*
Pause.
Cut to mid-shot of DAVE *at the wall, pissing and singing.*)

(*Cut to medium close-up of* EILEEN, *front view.*)

EILEEN: Oh suffering Jesus! That's all we need – you singing. As if life isn't purgatory enough without that.

(*The sound of torrential pissing.*)

DAVE: (*Voice over, singing*) '. . . a lazy river in the noonday sun . . .'

GRAN: (*Voice over*) Eileen! It's late!

EILEEN: Isn't this lively? (*To* GRAN, *placatory*) OK, Gran – we won't be much longer . . . (*To* DAVE) Come on dead hake! Hurry up! And be quiet.

(DAVE *comes into shot, singing, but very tired.*

Cut to medium close-up, two shot of EILEEN *and* DAVE, *back view. They go towards the house. Track with them.*)

GRAN: (*Voice over*) Eileen! Make sure that door's locked!

(DAVE *wobbly on his feet.*)

EILEEN: Wouldn't this put years on you? (*To* GRAN) OK, Gran.

(*They get to the door.* EILEEN *opens it, pushes* DAVE *inside.*)

I'm sure I was put on this earth just to be tormented.

(*Bangs door shut.*

Fade to white.

Soundtrack: The sound of DAVE *knocking something over and their feet on the stairs.*)

(*An intense whisper as Dave falls upstairs, voice over*) Be careful!

(DAVE *continues singing.*)

Oh, she's gonna have a right gob on her tomorrow.

(*Fade from white to:*)

INT. EILEEN AND DAVE'S FLAT IN GRAN'S HOUSE. NIGHT

EILEEN *and* DAVE *in wide shot at the table, eating.*

A fire is lit.

Hold.

Soundtrack: on the radio, Take It from Here.

Cut to close-up of EILEEN *at the table. She is eating.*

Soundtrack from Take It from Here *continued.*

JUNE WHITFIELD: (*Voice over*) Ooh Ron! Beloved!

(*Laughter.*

EILEEN *stops eating and looks at* DAVE.

Cut to close-up of DAVE *at table, eating loudly.*)

DICK BENTLEY: (*Voice over*) Yes Eth?
   (*Laughter.*
   Cut to close-up of EILEEN.
   Soundtrack: Fade Take It from Here *so that it is vaguely in the background.*)
EILEEN: Have you got to make that noise when you eat?
   (*Cut to close-up of* DAVE.)
DAVE: (*Making a noise while he eats*) What noise?
   (*Cut to close-up of* EILEEN.)
EILEEN: God blimey! What a future I've got to look forward to –
   twenty-five years with Mouth Almighty.
   (*Cut to medium close-up of door of flat. It opens.* UNCLE TED *is standing in the doorway carrying a candle at waist height so that his face is lit from directly beneath, making him look like a corpse. He switches off the light inside their flat.*)
UNCLE TED: (*In a sing-song voice*) I've switched the light off – I
   don't know whether I'm doing right or wrong-a!
   (*Slowly he closes the door.*
   Cut to two shot. EILEEN *and* DAVE *sitting at the table in the firelight. They have both stopped eating.*)
DAVE: (*Really scared*) Who the bleeding hell was that?
EILEEN: (*A little scared too*) Uncle Ted – my Dad's brother.
DAVE: God blimey – what a family I've married into – crowd of
   nutters. He frightened the bleeding life out of me!
   (*Soundtrack: the* Take It from Here *signature-tune heard.*
   Cut to:)

INT. HALL AND STAIRS. GRAN'S HOUSE. NIGHT
Wide shot from the bottom of the stairs. Darkness except for a candle held by UNCLE TED. *He comes downstairs.*
Soundtrack: BBC serial announcer: This is The Man in Black.
Footsteps echoing in time with UNCLE TED *descending the stairs.*
UNCLE TED *gets to the bottom of the stairs and is met by* GRAN *who is going into the kitchen.*
GRAN: (*Stern*) Teddy! Stop acting soft!
   (*She blows the candle out with a single, very definite blow.*
   Blackness.
   Cut to:)

[125]

EXT. ALLEY LEADING TO GRAN'S HOUSE. DAY
Late afternoon, the following Saturday. Hot summer's day.
Mid-wide shot. MOTHER *sits on a chair just inside the open door, left of frame. To the right of frame is* MAISIE'S *pram by the railings which lead to cellar steps and the cellar. Above this area is the parlour window which is half open.*
MOTHER *gently rocks the pram and fans herself with a newspaper. Pause and hold. Then* GRAN, *with a face like thunder, comes out followed by* EILEEN. GRAN *walks past* MOTHER *but neither of them speak.*

GRAN: (*Walking towards camera*) If you want me I'll either be at May Tobin's or in The Grapes.

EILEEN: In Phythian Street?

GRAN: (*Walking off camera*) Yer.

EILEEN: (*Calling after her*) Hey Gran – have you got a shilling for two tanners?
(*Cut to mid shot.* GRAN *from* EILEEN'S *point of view.*)

GRAN: (*Not turning around*) There's enough money in the meter.
(*She walks away down the alley and into the back entrance of an adjoining tenement building. As* GRAN *walks down the alley she passes* MAISIE, *but they don't speak.* MAISIE *carries shopping. Cut to mid-wide shot.* MOTHER *and* EILEEN *on doorstep.*)

EILEEN: She never leaves enough gas and the bleeding thing always goes.

MOTHER: (*Looking in her purse*) Way-o. 'E are love – I've got one.
(*Gives a shilling to* EILEEN.)

EILEEN: Thanks Mam.
(MAISIE *enters shot and joins them on the step.*)

MAISIE: Isn't she an auld cow? How can you live with her Ei?

EILEEN: Beggars can't be choosers Maisie – you know how hard it is to get a place of your own.

MOTHER: (*To* MAISIE) Did you get anything for a sarnie love?

MAISIE: Yer – I got a quarter of corned beef and a Hovis . . . oh and four Devon Delights.

EILEEN: (*Taking the shopping from* MAISIE) I've just made a pot of tea.
(EILEEN *goes inside the house.*)

MAISIE: (*Looking into the pram at the baby*) Has she been good Mam?

MOTHER: As good as gold.
>   (MOTHER *fans herself with the paper.* MAISIE *looks into the pram and rocks it.*
>   *Track away from them and into the parlour window, left to right.*
>   *When window is in close-up, hold.*
>   *Soundtrack: BBC Radio football results, 1958/59 season.*
>   *Cut to:*)

INT. PARLOUR. GRAN'S HOUSE. DAY
Medium close-up. DAVE, *side view, listening to the results and marking his coupon.*
Soundtrack: The football results finish, the racing results start.
EILEEN: (*Voice over*) Any luck?
DAVE: (*Turning to her*) No. Couldn't pick my nose.
>   (*Cut to:*)

INT. PARLOUR. MUM'S HOUSE. SAME SATURDAY. DAY
Close-up, side view of TONY, *listening to the racing results.*
Footsteps heard.
Soundtrack:
MOTHER: (*Voice over*) We're back!
TONY: Any pea wack Mam?
MOTHER: (*Voice over*) Yer – I've made a pan.
MAISIE: (*Voice over*) Did you back the winner?
TONY: With the donkeys I do? It had three legs. It's probably
>   still running.
>   (*Cut to:*)

EXT. GAUMONT CINEMA. NIGHT
Mid-wide shot.
Heavy rain. Queue waiting to get into cinema for the second house. The bottom of the frame is filled with black umbrellas.
Soundtrack from 'Guys and Dolls'.
Begin to crane up from the umbrellas in the cinema queue over the exterior of the cinema.
On the wall two posters are seen. On the left marked 'All This Week' is the poster for Love is a Many-Splendoured Thing.
On the right marked 'Coming Soon' the poster for Guys and Dolls.

Soundtrack: theme tune 'Love is a Many-Splendoured Thing'.
Dissolve to:

INT. GAUMONT CINEMA. NIGHT
Continue craning up over rows of people watching the film on the screen until MAISIE *and* EILEEN *are framed in medium close-up two shot, head on. Soundtrack:* 'Love is a Many-Splendoured Thing' *throbs out. The two girls weeping profusely.*

INT. WAREHOUSE. DAY
Low-angle shot looking straight up at a glass roof.
In slow motion two bodies come crashing through it. They are
GEORGE *and* TONY.
Soundtrack:
EILEEN: (*Voice over*) Wasn't that marvellous?
 (*Cut to:*)

INT. HOSPITAL CORRIDOR. NIGHT
Wide shot. MAISIE *running frantically down the corridor towards the camera.*
MAISIE: (*Voice over*) When he dies and she ran up that hill – I
 thought I was going to cry my eyes out.
 (*Cut to:*)

INT. HOSPITAL WARD. NIGHT
Two shot. Medium close-up. Side view of bed. MAISIE, *full faced, is lit.* GEORGE, *in profile, is not, so that he is in silhouette.*
MAISIE *holds* GEORGE's *right hand in hers. He is heavily bandaged and sedated and drifts in and out of sleep.*
MAISIE *is very upset.*
MAISIE: (*Cradling his hand in hers and very close to tears*) How are
 you love?
 (*Silence.*)
GEORGE: (*With great difficulty*) We fell off the bleeding scaffolding
 May . . .
 (*She just looks at him.*)
MAISIE: (*Trying not to cry*) Anything for notice . . .
 (GEORGE *drifts back into unconsciousness.* MAISIE, *unable to control herself any longer, breaks down and sobs.*)

(*Through sobs*) Oh George! George!
(*Hold.*
Soundtrack: Tommy Riley plays 'Galway Bay' on the
harmonica.
Crane up and around into the hospital window. Outside, it is
pouring with rain.
Hold on window.
Then without a dissolve crane back down and around to the first
camera position, side view, medium close-up of hospital bed, only
this time it is Tony's bed.
At his bedside MOTHER, EILEEN, ROSE *and* DAVE, *all very*
upset. TONY *is heavily bandaged and sedated. He is in*
silhouette. They are lit.)
MOTHER: (*Very upset*) Oh Tony! Oh son!
(*Soundtrack: Tommy Riley on the harmonica continues.*)

INT. KITCHEN. MOTHER'S HOUSE. MORNING OF
TONY'S WEDDING DAY

Medium close-up, two shot. MOTHER *and* MAISIE. MOTHER *facing*
camera, MAISIE *with her back to it.*
MAISIE *is fixing a carnation to* MOTHER'*s coat. She is having*
difficulty in pinning it on.
MOTHER: They're dead fiddly these, aren't they?
(*Cut to medium close-up, two shot.* MOTHER *and* MAISIE.)
MAISIE: Yer . . . did you get the carnations from Annie Gaffney?
(*Cut to medium close-up, two shot.* MOTHER *and* MAISIE.)
MOTHER: Yer.
MAISIE: (*Finishing*) The' are.
(*Cut to:*)

INT. PARLOUR. MOTHER'S HOUSE. THE MORNING OF
TONY'S WEDDING DAY

Medium close-up. GEORGE *at the window, back to camera.*
Pause.
Silence. Then GEORGE *turns around to camera.*
GEORGE: (*To* TONY) Well – aul' arse – are you ready?
(*Cut to mid shot.* TONY *sitting in Dad's chair next to the fireplace*
from GEORGE'*s point of view.*
TONY *stands up. He wears a caliper.*)

[129]

TONY: (*Clapping his hands together nervously*) Fighting fit!
(*Cut to mid-shot. Parlour door from* TONY'*s point of view.*
MOTHER *and* MAISIE *enter from the right,* EILEEN *and* DAVE
from the left. They all have their coats on and are wearing
buttonholes.)
MAISIE: (*To* TONY) Well – let's be having you!
MOTHER: (*To all*) Are we all ready?
(EILEEN *walks off camera right, to* TONY.
Cut to mid-shot from GEORGE'*s point of view of* TONY.
EILEEN *walks into shot.*)
EILEEN: (*To* TONY) Well – sun-bun – mustn't keep the bride
waiting.
(TONY (*very nervous, very uncomfortable*) *fiddles with his collar*
then puts his hands in his pockets.)
TONY: Oh God blimey – I'd never live it down.
(*Cut to mid-shot of parlour door from* TONY'*s point of view.*
They all exit – TONY *last.*
Hold on door.
Soundtrack: EILEEN *singing 'From the Candy Store on the*
Corner'.
Cut to:)

INT. CHURCH. MORNING OF TONY'S WEDDING DAY
Medium close-up. TONY *and* GEORGE *at the altar rails, backs to the*
camera.
Hold.
Soundtrack: EILEEN *singing. Then* GEORGE *and* TONY *turn around*
and look up the aisle, directly at camera.
Cut to medium close-up. Two shot. ROSE *and* MR FORSYTH, *her*
father, walking down the aisle towards the camera from TONY'*s and*
GEORGE'*s point of view.* ROSE *is wearing a white wedding dress*
and veil. The veil is very heavy so that she is almost invisible behind
it.
Cut to low-angle, two shot of TONY *and* ROSE *seen from behind.*
Crane up to medium close-up three shot of TONY *and* ROSE, *backs to*
camera, and PRIEST, *facing camera, conducting the marriage*
service.
Hold as they exchange vows.
Soundtrack: EILEEN *singing.*

[130]

Cut to mid-shot of pews. MOTHER, MAISIE, EILEEN *and* DAVE *in the front one – other relatives, including* GRAN, *behind, watching the wedding ceremony.*
A mixture of happiness tinged with sadness.
Cut to two shot, medium close-up of TONY *and* ROSE *at the altar rails from* PRIEST's *point of view.*
Wedding service continues.
Applause from wedding guests.
Cut to:

EXT. CHURCH. MORNING OF TONY'S WEDDING DAY
Wide shot.
TONY *and* ROSE *come out of the church followed by both families and they arrange themselves on the church steps for a group photo.*
MOTHER *slightly behind* TONY.
Family tableau.
They all pose for the photographer. They all smile. Then MOTHER's *face crumbles into tears.*
Soundtrack: MOTHER *singing 'Thanks to You'.*
Dissolve to:

INT. PARLOUR. ROSE'S PARENTS' HOUSE.
TONY'S WEDDING. NIGHT
MOTHER *in close-up surrounded by wedding guests continues song.*

EXT. ROSE'S PARENTS' HOUSE.
TONY'S WEDDING. NIGHT
Medium close-up. TONY *standing on the doorstep – hands in pockets – listening to his* MOTHER *singing. He begins to weep.*
Soundtrack: MOTHER *singing.*
TONY *now weeping uncontrollably.*
Soundtrack: MOTHER *singing last verse of song.*
Wedding guests applaud.
TONY's *weeping subsides but he continues just to stand there.*
Soundtrack: MR FORSYTH *singing 'I got into a Boxing Ring with a Fella Named Big-nosed Jim':*
RITCHIE: (*Voice over*) Oh hey Dad – you're not gonna sing that auld bleeding thing are you?
(*Whoops and laughter.*)

CATHY: (*Voice over*) Come on, let's have some records.
    (*Pause.*
    Then Oh Mein Papa, *played by Eddie Calvert, is heard.*
    Hold on TONY.
    Soundtrack: Fade wedding sounds.
    Fade in:)
TONY: (*Voice over*) Your dad enjoyed himself.
ROSE: (*Voice over*) I think everyone did.
TONY: (*Voice over*) Yer – it was a good do, wasn't it?
ROSE: (*Voice over*) Yer – but your Mam got a bit upset.
TONY: (*Voice over*) Arh – don't be worrying. She'll be all right.
    (*Dissolve to:*)

EXT. STREET OUTSIDE ROSE'S PARENTS' HOUSE.
TONY'S WEDDING. NIGHT

Mid shot, side view looking up the street. People come streaming out of the house. TONY *and* ROSE *at their head, followed by* MOTHER, MAISIE, EILEEN, GEORGE *and* DAVE, *and* ROSE's *family.*
Pan with them to taxi, which draws up. TONY *and* ROSE *get into the taxi, everyone waving their goodbyes. The taxi moves off into the darkness.*
Track with it and fade to black.
Soundtrack: 'O Waly, Waly', sung by an unaccompanied soprano in the arrangement by Benjamin Britten:

> 'The water is wide I cannot get o'er
> And neither have I wings to fly
> Give me a boat that will carry two
> Then both shall row my love and I . . .'

Dissolve to threequarter angle shot of both families waving to the taxi. They all go back into the house.
Dissolve to mid-shot, side view, looking down the street. MOTHER, MAISIE, GEORGE, DAVE *and* EILEEN *coming out of the house with their coats on. They say their goodbyes to* MR *and* MRS FORSYTH *and family.*
Soundtrack: 'O Waly, Waly' continued:

> 'Down in the meadow the other day
> A-gathering flowers both fine and gay
> A-gathering flowers both red and blue
> I little thought what love can do . . .'

MOTHER *and her family walk down the street into the darkness.*
Pan with them, then track with them and fade to black.
Dissolve to:

EXT. ALLEY. LEADING TO GRAN'S HOUSE.
TONY'S WEDDING. NIGHT

EILEEN *and* DAVE, *mid-shot, back view, walking towards the house.*
Soundtrack:

DAVE: (*Voice over*) Goodnight Nell.
MOTHER: (*Voice over*) Goodnight Dave.
EILEEN: (*Voice over*) See you tomorrow Mam.
MOTHER: (*Voice over*) OK Ei . . .

   ('*O Waly, Waly*' *continued:*)
       'I leaned my back up against some oak
       Thinking that it was a trusty tree.
       But first it bended and then it broke
       And so did my false love to me . . .'

   (DAVE *and* EILEEN *continue to walk towards the house. Track*
   with them into the darkness and fade to black.
   Dissolve to:)

EXT. STREET. LEADING TO MOTHER'S HOUSE.
TONY'S WEDDING. NIGHT

Mid-long shot. Back view of MAISIE, MOTHER *and* GEORGE,
MOTHER *walking slightly behind them.*
Track with them.
Soundtrack: '*O Waly, Waly*' *continued:*
       'A ship there is and she sails the sea
       She's loaded deep as deep can be
       But not so deep as the love I'm in
       I know not if I sink or swim . . .'

MAISIE *and* GEORGE *stop and look back at* MOTHER.
MAISIE: (*To* MOTHER) Come on Mam.
GEORGE: (*To* MOTHER) Come on girl.

   (MOTHER *walks between them. They all link arms and continue*
   walking down the street.
   Continue tracking with them into the dark.
   Track stops and they recede into the darkness.
   Then fade to black.

Hold on black.
Soundtrack: 'O Waly, Waly' continued:
 'O love is handsome and love is fine
 And love's a jewel while it is new
 But when it is old
 It groweth cold
 Then fades away like morning dew.'
(*Hold on darkness.*
Silence.
Fade up end credits.)

The Long Day Closes

The cast and crew of *The Long Day Closes* are as follows:

MOTHER	Marjorie Yates
BUD	Leigh McCormack
KEVIN	Anthony Watson
JOHN	Nicholas Lamont
HELEN	Ayse Owens
FRANCES	Joy Blakeman
JEAN	Denise Thomas
AMY	Patricia Morrison
EDNA	Tina Malone
CURLY	Jimmy Wilde
MR NICHOLLS	Robin Polley
MR BUSHELL	Peter Ivatts
BILLY	Gavin Mawdsley
LABOURER/CHRIST	Kirk McLaughlin
BLACK MAN	Marcus Heath
NUN	Victoria Davies
NURSE	Brenda Skeggs
ALBIE	Karl Skeggs
1ST BULLY	Lee Blennerhassett
2ND BULLY	Peter Hollier
3RD BULLY	Jason Jevons

Written and Directed by	Terence Davies
Producer	Olivia Stewart
Director of Photography	Michael Coulter
Production Designer	Christopher Hobbs
Editor	William Diver
Costume Designer	Monica Howe
Art Director	Kate Naylor
Music Director	Robert Lockhart

A British Film Institute and Channel 4 (Film Four International) Production, 1992

Liverpool 1955–1956

Fade up on black.
First titles then main title: 'The Long Day Closes'.
Fade out main titles.
Fade up on:

EXT. STREET. NIGHT
Close shot. A brick wall at the end of the street. It is pouring with rain.
Crane down over bricks, past a street sign which reads 'Kensington Street L5' *to a cinema poster for the Palladium cinema advertising* 'The Robe (*the first cinemascope film ever made*)'. *The poster is pasted directly on to the bricks and is tattered and torn.*
Soundtrack: The 20th-Century-Fox logo theme is heard. Track back and pan to wide shot of street. Continuous rain.
The street is a terraced one. On the right-hand side – three storey houses with cellars and railings in front of them. On the left-hand side – two-storey houses. All the houses are derelict. The street empty. Windows smashed, tattered curtains billowing, debris everywhere. Continuous rain.
Hold on this wide shot.
Soundtrack from The Ladykillers.
Track very slowly down the centre of the street.
Soundtrack: Cross fade to Nat King Cole singing 'Stardust'.
Continue track.
Continuous rain.
Soundtrack: Cross fade to the sound of a gong from The Happiest Days of Your Life: *Margaret Rutherford voice over:* 'Tap, Gossage, I said "tap" – you're not introducing a film.'
As we get half-way down the street track around to the right and into one of the derelict houses. Continuous rain inside the house.
Soundtrack from The Ladykillers: *Alec Guinness voice over:* 'Mrs Wilberforce? I understand that you have rooms to let?'
Cross fade to 'Meet Me in St Louis'.
Continue tracking into the hallway and crane up the stairs.
Continuous rain inside the house.

Crane and track stop half-way up the stairs.
Dissolve to:

INT. HALL AND STAIRCASE. DAY

The same camera position half-way up the stairs. The house is no longer derelict but bathed in brilliant sunshine from an internal skylight, open bedroom windows and open front door.

Bud, a boy of eleven, sits on the stairs, half bored. He plays with his shoelaces, his chin on his knees.

BUD: (*Calling*) Mam! . . . Mam! . . .
   (*Silence.*)
   Can I go to the pictures, Mam?
   (*Silence. Her footsteps are heard. He races downstairs. Cut to:*)

INT. HALLWAY. DAY

Foot of the stairs. Mid-wide shot.

BUD *comes rushing to the foot of the stairs.*

MOTHER *comes up the hall towards camera from the back yard and goes into the kitchen, which is opposite the stairs.*

BUD: Mam.

MOTHER: (*Going into kitchen*) Yer?

BUD: I've got a penny.

MOTHER: (*Voice over from the kitchen*) So?

BUD: If you gave me elevenpence I'd have a shilling.

MOTHER: (*Coming out of the kitchen and going down the hall and into the yard*) You're not soft, are you?

BUD: (*Leaning over the banister and calling after her*) Arh, go on Mam
   . . . Mam!
   (*Silence.*)
   Our Titchie said she'd take me . . .
   (*Silence.*)
   Mam . . . Arh . . . go on Mam . . .
   (*Silence.*)

MOTHER: (*Voice over, from the yard*) Eh Bud – will you get me those nets from the lads' bedroom?
   (*Pause.*)

BUD: (*His voice drenched in boredom*) OK Mam . . .
   (*Lethargically he goes upstairs, trailing his hand along the banister.*

Hold on empty stairs.
Cut to:)

EXT. BACK BEDROOM WINDOW. DAY
From the outside close-up of BUD *kneeling at the open window, nets in his hands. Bright sunshine.*
MOTHER: (*Voice over from the yard*) Oh, come on, lad! Where's
  those nets? I want to wash them.
  (*He drops the nets on to her.*
  Cut to:)

EXT. BACK YARD. DAY
High shot of MOTHER *in yard – from* BUD'S *point of view directly overhead.* MOTHER *is hanging out washing as the nets descend on her, covering her head.*
Cut to close-up side view of MOTHER, *the nets descending over her head.*
MOTHER: (*Taking the nets from her head*) That's before he'll bring
  them down . . .
  (*Cut to high shot of* MOTHER *from* BUD'S *point of view.*
  Looking up and pretending to be annoyed) You little bugger!
  (*Cut to:)*

EXT. BACK BEDROOM WINDOW. DAY
Close-up of BUD *at back-bedroom window, head on from the outside. He giggles. Laughter and shouting is heard and he looks up. The smile fading from his face.*
Cut to:

EXT. GARAGE WALL. DAY
BUD'S *point of view of Smitten's Garage. The garage lies beyond the back-yard wall.*
Three labourers are building a wall. All are stripped to the waist and very muscular, one in particular. They are lifting bags of cement over their heads. A bag bursts, showering one of them with powdered cement. They all roar with laughter. One of the labourers – the particularly muscular one – looks up at BUD *and waves and smiles at him.*
Cut to:

INT. BACK BEDROOM. DAY

Mid shot back of BUD. *He comes back inside the room and squats on the floor beside and below the window. He looks back at the open window and the labourers' laughter can still be heard. He then puts his face to his knees. He looks faintly, vaguely disturbed. Hold.*
Dissolve to:

INT. CHURCH. LATE AFTERNOON

Close-up of one of the Stations of the Cross. Christ on his way to Calvary but depicted in High Victorian Catholic revival.
Cut to close-up high shot looking down of BUD *performing the Stations of the Cross. He blesses himself and starts silently to pray. Pause. He stops praying and looks up.*
Cut to special effects shot of BUD's *point of view, but it is not the Station of the Cross he saw. It is a big close-up of the right hand of Christ being nailed to the cross.*
Cut to close-up of BUD *as he drops his joined hands and stares straight up.*
Cut to special effects shot of close-up of Christ's hand. They finish hammering the nail in. Hold. The hand quivers then is still. Then as we track back and crane up the cross begins to turn so that eventually as the camera rises above it and comes to rest the whole of the cross and Christ crucified are revealed – only we are above and looking down on to them. Christ and the cross are suspended at a terrible height. Below the cross is infinite black space.
Hold.
This Christ is young and handsome and muscular. Pause. Then Christ looks up at the camera and BUD. *It is the labourer at the garage. Slowly he grins then barks a terrifying human bark at* BUD.
Cut to close-up of BUD. *He jumps out of his skin, then, realizing where he is, he bows his head and resumes his praying in the unbroken quiet of the silent, dark church.*
Soundtrack of MOTHER *singing from the yard 'If You Were the Only Girl in the World'.*
Dissolve to:

INT. HALL. DAY

Shot of BUD *coming down and sitting on stairs. Looking through the banisters.* MOTHER's *singing continues.*

[140]

Cut to:

INT. HALL AND STAIRS. DAY

Shot of Mum through banisters. She comes up the hall from the yard and goes into the kitchen, continuing to sing softly.
Cut to:

INT. STAIRS. DAY

Close-up of BUD *sitting on the stairs looking at* MOTHER *in the kitchen as she sings.*
Cut to:

INT. KITCHEN. DAY

Close-up, side view, of MOTHER *from* BUD's *point of view. She is making an egg custard. She stops singing.*
Silence. She stands there rolling pastry with a sterilized milk bottle. Pause. Then she looks towards the stairs and BUD *and smiles.*
MOTHER: Go on . . . get me purse.
BUD: (*Voice over*) Arh, thanks Mam!
　　(*She goes back to rolling pastry and humming softly to herself. Hold. Then:*)

INT. KITCHEN/LEAN-TO. DAY

Track and pan right to left to half-open window opposite MOTHER. KEVIN *is seen through the window, bent over the sink in the lean-to washing himself. He is stripped to the waist. He stands up into shot and begins to get dry.*
MOTHER: (*Voice over*) Your tea's ready, Kev.
KEVIN: OK, Mam.
　　(*Continue track and pan right to left to kitchen door.* JOHN *and* HELEN *are coming down the hall.*
　　HELEN *goes half-way up the stairs and* JOHN *stops at the door.*)
HELEN: (*Leaning over the banister*) Hey John, will you get the flat irons out for me?
JOHN: (*Taking off his coat and rummaging in the space below the stairs*) OK, Titch.
HELEN: (*Running upstairs*) Hi yer, Mam!
JOHN: Where's our Bud, Mam?
MOTHER: (*Walking out of kitchen to lean-to*) The pictures – where else?

(Soundtrack: the orchestral introduction to 'At Sundown' from Love Me or Leave Me *sung by Doris Day.*
Cut to:)

EXT. CINEMA. EARLY EVENING

The Hippodrome picture house advertising Love Me or Leave Me. *It is pouring with rain. Wide shot of the side of the building which has a series of exit doors running down its entire length.* BUD *is standing inside one of them sheltering from the rain.*
Soundtrack: Doris Day sings 'At Sundown' from Love Me or Leave Me.
A man passes by BUD.
BUD: *(Offering him his money)* Take us in, Mister?
   (The man hurries by without responding.
   Soundtrack of Doris Day continued.
   It starts to get dark.
   BUD *still waits and tries to keep warm and dry. A couple pass.)*
BUD: Will you take us in, please?
   (They hurry by without answering.
   Soundtrack: Doris Day.
   A second man walks by and off camera right.)
BUD: Will you take us in, Mister?
MAN: *(Voice over)* OK, come on then.
BUD: Arh, thanks Mister!
   *(*BUD *runs off, camera right. Hold.*
   Soundtrack: Doris Day singing. Continued.
   Orchestral interlude in song. Hold on empty frame.
   The rain stops. It is now completely dark.)

EXT. CINEMA. NIGHT

Track in on cinema.
Soundtrack: Doris Day sings end of song.
Continue track right to left as all the doors of the cinema open and the audience comes streaming out. The stalls seats can be seen immediately beyond the doors. BUD *is amongst the crowd. He walks into a close shot. He begins to run and as he passes another boy, he sings sarcastically to him.*
BUD: 'Tiddle – iddle – iddle
      Tiddle – iddle – iddle

[142]

Tiddle – iddle – iddle Hodge!'

TIDDLE HODGE: (*Voice over*) I'll get you Mavis!
    (*Continue tracking with* BUD *right to left as he runs away.
    Dissolve to:*)

INT. HALLWAY. BONFIRE NIGHT

Side view of BUD *in medium close-up as he walks slowly down the
hall. Track with him right to left.*
Soundtrack: Sound of BUD *running down the hall.*
MOTHER: (*Voice over*) What are you running for?
BUD: (*Voice over*) (*Breathless*) Tiddle Hodge was chasing me.
MOTHER: (*Voice over*) Why?
BUD: (*Voice over*) I was skitting him.
MOTHER: (*Voice over*) You be careful – one day he'll catch you
    and give you a right go-along.
    (*The house and hall are dark but are lit from the light from the
    bonfire outside in the street. The whole hall is aflame.
    Dissolve to:*)

INT. PARLOUR. BONFIRE NIGHT

Continue tracking with BUD *in medium close-up, right to left.*
Everything is flame-coloured.
BUD: (*Moving to the window and looking out*) Tiddle – iddle – iddle
    – Hodge.
    (*The sound of the bonfire, fireworks and people. Track stops
    when he gets to the window. He looks out through the nets.
    Cut to:*)

EXT. STREET. BONFIRE NIGHT

BUD'S *point of view. The bonfire is surrounded and thronged with
people and children from the street.*
Directly opposite BUD'S *point of view one man is standing by the
bonfire, laughing and talking. He is short but very powerfully built.
His shirt is collarless and open on the chest. His shirt sleeves have been
rolled up as far as they will go.*
Cut to close shot of window with BUD'S *face in it behind the nets. He
stares at the man for a long time.*
Cut to:

[143]

INT. PARLOUR. BONFIRE NIGHT

Side view close-up of BUD *staring at the man. Slowly* BUD *sinks down until only his chin touches the window sill on which his arms are crossed. Everything is flame-coloured.*
Soundtrack of Kathleen Ferrier singing 'Blow The Wind Southerly'.
Dissolve to:

EXT. STREET. DAY

Side or three-quarter back view of BUD *as he runs to school. He is late. Track with him right to left. He passes the bottoms of three streets. At each street bonfires are smouldering from the night before.*
Soundtrack of Kathleen Ferrier singing:

> 'They told me last night there were
> ships in the offing
> And I hurried down to the deep
> rolling sea
> But my eyes could not see it
> wherever might be it
> The barque that is bearing
> my lover to me . . .'

Cut to:

EXT. SCHOOL. DAY

High shot looking in through the window at BUD.
On the outside of the school track into 'Board Schools' and 'Junior Boys', chiselled into the sandstone façade.
Cut to:

INT. CLASSROOM. DAY

All the children are working quietly. Pause. The rest of the classroom goes dark and motionless. Only BUD *is lit. He looks up.*
Soundtrack, Kathleen Ferrier singing:

> 'Blow the wind southerly, southerly, southerly
> Blow balmy breeze o'er the bonny blue sea . . .'

He looks to his right out of the school window.
Dissolve to BUD'S *point of view of window. But instead of seeing the Liverpool skyline he sees a huge sailing ship moving across the frame right to left. It sails in slow motion through huge, heavy seas, wind and rain.*

Soundtrack of Kathleen Ferrier singing:
>'Blow the wind southerly, southerly, southerly
>Blow balmy breeze and bring him to me . . .'

Cut to close-up of BUD. *Wind and rain on his face and hair. He gasps as he tries to keep gazing at the ship.*
Cut to:

SAILING SHIP

Wind and rain in the rigging as the ship glides from right to left across frame. The storm still raging, still lashing the ship.
Soundtrack, Kathleen Ferrier singing:
>'Is it not sweet to hear the breeze singing
>As like he is come o'er the deep
>>rolling sea . . .'

The ship passes from view and fades.
Cut to:

INT. CLASSROOM. DAY

Front view close-up of BUD *at desk. The storm subsides. He keeps looking for the ship.*
Soundtrack, Kathleen Ferrier singing:
>'But sweeter and dearer by far 'tis
>When bringing the barque of my true love
>>in safety to me.'

The lights go back on.
He turns away from the window. A look of infinite disappointment comes over his face. His head drops. He and the other children go back to work as the lesson continues.
A triangle of vertical white light from a cinema projection booth appears above their heads.
Soundtrack: 'Carousel Waltz'. Hold. Then track and pan left to right from BUD *at desk to front of classroom but instead of seeing the teacher at her desk, dissolve to:*

INT. CINEMA. NIGHT

Pan left to right to MOTHER, BUD *and* HELEN *in close three shot in the balcony of a cinema – the sort that has been converted from a theatre.* BUD, *sitting between* MOTHER *and* HELEN, *leans on the*

parapet. *They are watching 'Carousel'. The projection light is above their heads.*
Hold for a moment.
Soundtrack: 'Carousel Waltz'. Then crane down from three shot in balcony and then dissolve to:

EXT. FAIRGROUND. NIGHT

Crane down to two shot of MOTHER *and* HELEN.
HELEN: There's our John and Kevin, Mam.
MOTHER AND HELEN: (*Calling*) Kev! John!
    (*Continue crane down to* BUD *in close-up.*)
BUD: (*Calling*) John! Kevin!
    (*And track away left to right.*
    Soundtrack: 'Carousel Waltz' begins to fade. Fade all natural sound.
    Dissolve to track left to right to two shot of KEVIN *and* JOHN *in side view. They are holding rifles and are firing them and laughing – they haven't heard the calls.*
    Soundtrack: A man singing 'She Moved Through the Fair', a cappella.
      'My young love said to me "My mother
        won't mind
      And my father won't slight you
      For your lack of kind" – '
Dissolve to track left to right to BUD *in close-up eating candyfloss and following* MOTHER *and* HELEN. *Track with him as he walks left to right behind* MOTHER *and* HELEN. *He looks up at* MOTHER *and smiles.*
Soundtrack of MAN *singing:*
    'And she stepped away from me
    And this she did say
    It will not be long, love, 'til
      our wedding day'
Two shot of MOTHER *and* HELEN (*who is slightly in front of* MOTHER). MOTHER *and* HELEN *are eating candyfloss.*
MOTHER *looks back at* BUD *and smiles though no sound can be heard.*
Track with MOTHER *left to right as she moves beyond* HELEN *and* BUD, *into close-up. She looks radiant as she walks.*

Soundtrack of MAN *singing:*
>   'She stepped away from me
>   And she went thro' the fair
>   And fondly I watched her
>   Move here and move there
>   And then she went homeward
>   With one star awake
>   As the swan in the evening
>   Moves over the lake . . .'
Dissolve to:)

INT. PARLOUR. NIGHT

Pan to two shot of MOTHER *and* BUD *in an armchair, sitting in the firelight. Hold.*
Soundtrack of MAN *singing:*
>   'Last night she came to me,
>   She came softly in
>   So softly she came that
>   her feet made no din . . .'
As we track in on them.
Soundtrack: MAN's *voice becomes* MOTHER's *voice, singing:*
>   'And she laid her hand on
>   me and this she did say
>   "It will not be long, love,
>   till our wedding day".'
Track stops in mid close two shot. Long silence as they both sit there looking into the fire. BUD *snuggles up against* MOTHER *as she strokes his hair.*
MOTHER: (*More to herself*) My dad used to sing that.
BUD: Granddad O'Brien?
MOTHER: (*Her eyes filling with tears*) Yer.
   (*She continues stroking his hair – but crying silently so that* BUD *won't hear her or be disturbed. Hold on both of them as they sit in the firelight. Silence.*
   Cut to:)

INT. HALLWAY AND STAIRS. NIGHT

Wide shot of MOTHER *going upstairs.*
MOTHER: (*Dead beat*) Lock up, will you Kev?

[147]

KEVIN: (*Voice over*) OK, Mam.
  (*She moves slowly up the dark stairs. Hold on stairs.*
  Soundtrack: Tom Drake and Judy Garland from Meet Me in St
  Louis.
  (*Mother gone. Hold on empty dark stairs.*
  Cut to:)

INT. PARLOUR. NIGHT

Close-up on BUD *in firelight.*
Cut to two shot of KEVIN *and* FRANCES *from* BUD's *point of view on
the sofa which they have pulled in front of the fire.* FRANCES *is in the
foreground.* KEVIN *behind her. They both look at* BUD. FRANCES
talks softly to him. KEVIN *points at* BUD *then points to the ceiling
indicating bed for* BUD. KEVIN *caresses* FRANCES.
Cut to close-up of BUD *by sideboard. He looks crestfallen and moves to
the parlour door which is a curtain. Pan with him right to left.*
FRANCES: (*Voice over*) Goodnight Bud.
  (*He doesn't answer.*
  Cut to:)

INT. HALL. NIGHT

Close-up two shot of JOHN *and* JEAN *by the open front door in the
dark kissing and talking softly to each other.*
Soundtrack of Judy Garland singing.
The vestibule door slowly closes over on JOHN *and* JEAN *leaving their
silhouettes reflected behind the decorated glass.*
Cut to:

INT. HALL AND STAIRS. NIGHT

Shot of BUD *climbing softly, slowly up the dark stairs.*
BUD *disappears.*
Cut to:

INT. MAIN BEDROOM. NIGHT

*Shot of ceiling directly over main window. Outside it is raining
heavily. The window is reflected on the ceiling, it ripples like V-shaped
water.*
Cut to close-up side view of BUD *in bed. Outside it is raining heavily –
the rain being reflected on the wall by Bud's bed. He turns on his back*

and touches the rain's reflection on the wall.
Soundtrack: Judy Garland's singing continues.
BUD: (*Calling softly*) Mam! Mam!
    (*Cut to two shot of* MOTHER *and* HELEN *in bed asleep but*
    favour MOTHER.
    Soundtrack of Judy Garland singing.
    Absolute silence except for the rain.
    Cut to special effects shot top shot looking straight down on BUD
    in bed. The bed looks coffin-like. He lies perfectly still in the
    silence.
    Then a pair of hands – the hands of Christ/labourer complete
    with stigmata – come through the back wall behind the head of
    the bed and grasp BUD *around the head and face.* BUD *is*
    paralysed with fear.)
CHRIST/LABOURER: You're mine!
    (BUD *screams in terror.*
    Cut to BUD *sitting up into shot, screaming and screaming. Hands*
    enter shot and hold his face. Track back to two shot of MOTHER
    and BUD *on bed in side view,* MOTHER *holding* BUD *to her.* BUD
    is sobbing and sobbing, the rain reflected on the wall behind
    them.)
BUD: (*Sobbing*) It was a man. It was a *man!*
MOTHER: (*Calming him*) You're all right. You're all right . . .
    (*Pan left to right to bedroom floor. Rain reflected on it. Hold on*
    floor.
    Dissolve to:)

INT. PARLOUR. LATE AFTERNOON

Floor of parlour. The parlour window is reflected on the floor. It is
pouring with heavy rain. Hold on floor.
Soundtrack: Orchestral version of 'A Shropshire Lad'.
The rain stops. The sun comes out weakly, fades and comes out again
so that the reflection of the window on the floor appears and
disappears. A blazing fire in the grate. Hold on floor.
Then track and pan left to right to window to back close-up of BUD *at*
the window standing inside the nets looking out at the street. Odd
squalls of rain against the glass. BUD *sighs and kicks his foot and trails*
his fingers along the panes looking very bored. Hold on BUD.
Dissolve to:

EXT. STREET. LATE AFTERNOON

Medium close-up of BUD *at the window looking out. It is snowing and he looks excitedly at the falling snow. In the background a blazing fire bathes the whole of the dark parlour with warmth.* BUD *strains to look up at the sky and the falling snow.*

Soundtrack: 'A Shropshire Lad' ends.

He disappears from behind the nets into the dark, warm parlour.

BUD: (*Voice over*) What am I going to get for Christmas, Mam?

MOTHER: (*Voice over*) Don't be so nosey.

    (*Dissolve to:*)

INT. PARLOUR. LATE AFTERNOON/EARLY EVENING

Close-up of sideboard in parlour lit only by the blazing fire. Early evening. Pan right to left along sideboard. It is covered with fruit and Christmas cards. Continue panning right to left to fire in close-up. It blazes.

Dissolve/cut to:

INT. CLASSROOM. DAY

The end of the school nativity play. The play has taken place at one end of a classroom on the lower floor. It has been staged in front of the fireplace.

The Holy Family are already seated. Behind them desks and chairs form a semi-circle. Mary, seated behind a cradle, holds a doll – the baby Jesus. Joseph stands on her right. The rest of the class troop in as shepherds, the magi, angels.

CHILDREN: (*Singing*) 'Oh come all ye faithful
    Joyful and triumphant
    Oh come ye, oh come ye,
    To Beth-eth-le-hem . . .'

    (*As they sing, they arrange themselves on top of the desks and chairs. The angels take the highest position behind the Holy Family on the desks. The shepherds stand by Joseph's left.* BUD, *one of the shepherds, carries a crook with a lantern suspended from it.*)

CHILDREN: (*Singing*) 'Come and behold him
    Born the king of angels
    Oh come let us adore him
    Oh come let us adore him

Oh come let us adore him
Christ the Lord.'
(*A pause as they settle into a tableau. Then they start to sing
'Silent Night'.*)
CHILDREN: (*Singing*) 'Silent night, Holy night
All is calm, all is bright
Round yon virgin, mother and child
Holy infant so tender and mild . . .'
(BUD *looks at his* MOTHER *and smiles as he sings.
Cut to shot of group of mothers watching their children in the
play, all very proud.* BUD'S MOTHER *is in the middle of the
group. She looks at him and smiles but is choked with tears.*)
CHILDREN: (*Singing*) 'Sleep in heavenly peace
Sleep in heavenly peace.'
(*Cut to:*)

INT. HALL AND STAIRS. NIGHT
Mid-shot front view of BUD *sitting half-way up the stairs. The stairs
and hall are dark but he is lit from the brilliant light flooding from the
kitchen. Voices are heard in the kitchen – laughing and talking. Hold
on shot of* BUD. *He looks at them.*
Cut to:

INT. KITCHEN. NIGHT
BUD'S *point of view of his* MOTHER, HELEN, JOHN *and* KEVIN *in
the kitchen. They are talking about Christmas.*
Cut to:

INT. HALL AND STAIRS. NIGHT
Close-up front view of BUD *on the stairs. He smiles and looks towards
the front door. The light from the kitchen fades as do the voices of his
family and a light in front of him begins to flood his face. He smiles.
His face becoming radiant.*
*Soundtrack: Bing Crosby, Vera Ellen, Rosemary Clooney and Danny
Kaye singing 'White Christmas'.*
Dissolve to:

INT. HALLWAY. NIGHT
BUD'S *point of view of the dark hallway and front door.*

Soundtrack of 'White Christmas' continues.
The dark is gradually giving way to a wonderfully soft glowing light
as the whole of the front of the house opens up.
It is snowing outside and all Bud's family are dressed in red and white
Santa Claus outfits and miming to 'White Christmas'. They gather
themselves around a huge, decorated Christmas tree. They are singing
just for BUD.
Soundtrack of 'White Christmas' continues.
Dissolve to:

EXT. STREET AND BUD'S HOUSE. NIGHT
Mid long shot. Real time. Snow.
The family are no longer singing but the house is filled with people and
is a blaze of light in the midst of darkness. Someone has put a record of
'White Christmas' on the radiogram and everyone joins in.
Soundtrack: all sing 'White Christmas'.
Track away left to right down the street away from Bud's house.
Continue tracking through the snow and into the darkness. All real
sounds fade as we track over the dark house fronts. There is a sudden
wind and a flurry of snow.
Soundtrack: Orson Welles in The Magnificent Ambersons.
Continue tracking left to right into the darkness. Then crane up out of
darkness to a high shot of the main road. Fade up natural sound. The
main road is crammed with people doing the Hokey-Kokey. Traffic
has been stopped or slowed to a crawl.
All are singing 'The Kokey-Kokey'.
A VOICE: It's twelve o'clock!
>   (*Everyone begins shouting, kissing, wishing each other 'All the*
>   *best', 'Happy New Year'. People bang bats on the pavements,*
>   *bang pots and pan lids with spoons, car horns hoot, fog horns*
>   *bleat from the river.*)
ALL: (*Singing*) 'Should old acquaintance
>   be forgot
>   And never brought to mind
>   Should old acquaintance
>   be forgot
>   For the sake of Auld Lang Syne . . .'
>   (*Crane down to a small circle of people consisting of* MOTHER,
>   BUD, HELEN, JOHN *and* JEAN.)

[152]

ALL: (*Singing*) 'For Auld Lang Syne my dear
    For Auld Lang Syne
    We'll take a cup of
    Kindness yet
    For the sake of Auld Lang Syne.'

MOTHER: (*Kissing* BUD) All the best, Bud!

BUD: All the best, Mam!

    (*The rest do the same. Track and pan right to left away from them – past* KEVIN *and* FRANCES *kissing in a pub doorway to the darkness of the street. Fade all natural sound. Continue tracking right to left into the darkness then out of it. Out of the darkness emerges* MOTHER, BUD, HELEN, KEVIN *and* JOHN *walking down the street towards their house. Track slowly with them right to left.*)

BUD: (*To* MOTHER) What's 'Kinnershet', Mam?

MOTHER: What's what?

BUD: In that song . . . 'We'll take a cup of "Kinnershet"'.

MOTHER: Oh! It's 'kindness yet'.

NEIGHBOUR: All the best!

ALL: All the best, Frank! Happy New Year Mr Campbell!

    (*Track stops when they all reach the house. Medium-long shot front view of house. They all go in. The house lights have been left on.*)

MOTHER: Will you lock the back door, Kev?

KEVIN: I locked it before we went out.

JOHN: (*Resigned air*) You don't half panic, Mam.

    (*They all begin to drift upstairs except* MOTHER, *who closes the front door. The hall and parlour lights go off and we hear them troop upstairs. The house is dark except for the fairy lights on the Christmas tree in the parlour window, flashing on and off.* KEVIN *and* JOHN's *laughter and talk fades into silence as they drift into sleep. Silence.*)

MOTHER: (*Voice over*) Good night, Titch.

HELEN: (*Voice over*) Good night, Mam.

    (*Silence.*)

MOTHER: (*Voice over*) God help anyone with no home tonight.

    (*Silence. It starts to rain. Hold on the dark house. Pan down to street and snow. The rain turning the snow into a dirty slush.*)

[153]

MOTHER: (*Voice over*) Well, I wonder what 1956 'll bring.
(*Dissolve to:*)

INT. HEADMISTRESS'S STUDY. PRIMARY SCHOOL.
AFTERNOON

Two shot side view of BUD *seated and in front of him the*
HEADMISTRESS *who is a nun. Her face cannot be seen. Only her*
hands move as she bathes the back of BUD's *neck as he bends over.*

HEADMISTRESS: Stay here until your nose stops bleeding.

BUD: (*Bending his head right back*) Thank you, Sister.
(*Dissolve to shot of the study looking towards the window. The*
study is dark – made even darker by the brilliant sunshine
flooding in through the bay windows, sash bay windows from
floor to ceiling – fully opened. In front of the window, in the bay,
a large desk.)

TEACHER: (*Voice over*) Put something cold on his neck – like keys
– that'll do the trick.
(*Shot of* BUD *– his head still held back – walking towards the*
desk and open window. Track with him. Beyond the window but
directly outside it is the back school yard. At the far end of the
school yard is a strip of grass and a perimeter wall beyond that.
In the centre of the wall a permanently locked wooden door. To
the right of this door, a pear tree. The schoolchildren are not
allowed to play on this grass area. BUD *stops at the desk by the*
study window. He brings his head back up to see if his nose is still
bleeding. It isn't. Track continues. BUD *looks out the window at*
the children playing in the school yard. In a kind of unofficial
sports day – teams compete in sack race, three-legged race, egg
and spoon race, supervised by teachers. Parents look on.
Track past BUD.
Dissolve to track back from the open study window – only now
there is no desk. In its place is a piano in front of which is seated
a teacher – Miss Delaney. Her class is arranged in front of and
below the study window – in the school yard. BUD *included.*
Miss Delaney strikes a note. Her class hum it. She strikes the note
again. Again they hum. She begins to play. Continue track back.)

CHILDREN: (*Singing*) 'Faith of our Fathers sanctify my breast
Body of Christ be, now, my saving guest
Deep in thy wounds Lord hide and shelter me

[154]

So that I'll never, never part from thee.'
(*In front of the choir the rest of the schoolchildren are sitting
facing the choir, with their teachers. On either side the parents,
sitting on chairs, looking on. All very formal. Brilliant sunshine.
Choir fades. Continue track back.*
Dissolve to:)

EXT. BACK SCHOOL YARD. PRIMARY SCHOOL. AFTERNOON
*Shot of the grass area and the pear tree and the door in the perimeter
wall. Breeze in the pear tree.*
Track in on door for a moment then track stops.
Hold for a moment.
*Then the door in the perimeter wall opens of its own accord – debris
and the city beyond. Hold.*
Cut to:

EXT. SECONDARY SCHOOL. MORNING
Close-up (back view) of BUD. *It is his first day at secondary school. A
crisp cold morning. Boys everywhere. He walks towards the school
gates. Track with him. A boy walks past him then stops.*
FIRST BOY: (*To* BUD) Are you Povey?
    (BUD *shakes his head.* FIRST BOY *stops at school gates against
    which two other* BOYS *are leaning.*)
FIRST BOY: (*Laughing to the two others*) I thought he was Povey.
SECOND BOY: (*To* BUD) Are you from Bernard Street?
BUD: No – Canon Kennedy's.
    (*The three boys bar his entrance into the school yard. Then just
    stand looking at him. Track stops.*)
THIRD BOY: (*To* BUD) Who's a fruit then, eh?
    (*Cut to close-up front view of* BUD. *He is terrified.*
    Cut to:)

INT. MR NICHOLLS' CLASSROOM. DAY
Close-up of BUD *standing in a line which moves slowly from left to
right. Pan with him. He looks petrified.*
*Soundtrack: The sound of the cane as all the boys are systematically
beaten. It comes to Bud's turn. He holds out his hand. The sound of
the cane. He is caned. He is close to tears.*
Cut to shot of BUD *sitting down at one of the front desks. He is trying*

[155]

not to cry. Mr Nicholls brings the cane down hard on Bud's desk frightening him still further.

MR NICHOLLS: (*Voice over*) That's just to show you who's
boss . . .
(*Cut to close-up of* MR NICHOLLS.)

MR NICHOLLS: . . . I'm Mr Nicholls . . . you play ball with me,
I'll play ball with you.
(*Cut to:*)

INT. DINNER CENTRE. LUNCHTIME

Line of boys – BUD among them – moving towards the still where food is being served. Pan/track with them right to left side view. All the boys carry steel trays as they each in turn get their lunch at that still. Chaos. Terrible noise. BUD looks both bewildered and terrified. BUD gets served.

Cut to shot of BUD – from the other side of the still counter – getting served. Beyond him rows and rows of large trestle tables filled with boys eating. Chaos. Noise.

Cut to mid-shot side view of BUD. Pan/track with him right to left past row upon row of trestle tables, crowded with boys all eating their food rapidly and without relish. Terrible noise. BUD looking more and more demoralized. Track stops when he sits down at the end of a table and starts to eat. Just as he does so:

DINNER LADY: (*Voice over*) Seconds!
(*A mad scramble for more unappetizing food.*
BUD *sits there in the pandemonium just looking and picking at his food.*
Soundtrack: Noise of boys playing in playground, then the sound of a whistle.
Cut to:)

EXT. PLAYGROUND. AFTERNOON

Close-up of MR BUSHELL *with the whistle still in his mouth. He is the headmaster – short, spruce, correct. A military man. Silence as he eyes the entire playground. Pause. Then he blows his whistle.*

Cut to wide shot of boys standing where they stopped when the whistle blew.

MR BUSHELL: Get into line!
(*They all get into their respective class lines. Silence.*)

[156]

(*Blowing on his whistle*) S4! . . . Right wheel! Quick march!
. . . Left, right, left . . .
(*S4, Bud's class, go into the school. Line by line they go into the
school from the playground in absolute silence.*
Cut to:)

INT. CHURCH HIGH ALTAR. LATE AFTERNOON
*Wide shot from high altar looking up the body of the church.
Benediction has not yet begun. The church interior is dark. The pews
filling up rapidly and silently with boys from the whole school. They
genuflect at the pews before entering them. The last few boys settle in
pews. The whole church is full. Silence except for the odd cough.
Hold. Then the whole congregation rises.
Cut to mid shot of* BUD *in pew surrounded by the three boys he met on
his first day at secondary school.*
SECOND BOY: (*Imitating* BUD) I'm from Canon Kennedy!
THIRD BOY: Who's a fruit then, eh?
FIRST BOY: (*Laughing*) Povey!
    (BUD *is frightened.*
    All begin to sing the Tantum Ergo.)
ALL: (*Singing*) 'Tantum ergo sacramentum
       Veneremur cernui
       Et antiquum documentum
       Novo cedet ritui . . .

       Genitori genitoque
       Laus et jubilatio
       Salust honor virtus quoque
       Sit et benedictio . . .'
Soundtrack: Cross fade to:
HELEN: (*Voice over, a regular weekly ritual*) Well, did you get me
    stuff for me?
    (*Cut to:*)

INT. CHURCH CORRIDOR. LATE AFTERNOON
*Corridor running down the entire length of church. All the boys are
filling the corridor pushing towards the doors at the far end.* BUD *in
close-up amid the seething mass of boys. Crane with him as he looks
back over his shoulder anxiously.*
Soundtrack:

[157]

BUD: (*Voice over*) Yer – two pairs of nylons – 15 denier. American Tan, fully fashioned – Panstick, nail varnish . . .

HELEN: (*Voice over*) Majestic Red?

BUD: (*Voice over*) Yer . . . Imperial Leather and the Picture Goer and Picture Show . . .

(*Dissolve to:*)

INT. BUD'S HOUSE. EARLY EVENING

Track back with BUD *in close-up from the dark hall to the bright kitchen. The kitchen seems magical and bright to* BUD. *He is in the midst of a sea of pastel-coloured dresses – coming in from the dark hall to the bright kitchen. He is surrounded by* FRANCES, JEAN *and* AMY *but only the dresses are seen.*

HELEN: (*Voice over*) Evening in Paris?

BUD: They didn't have any.

AMY: (*Voice over*) 'e' are Titch – you can have a bit of mine.

(*Pan to wide shot. Girls –* FRANCES, JEAN *and* AMY *walk into shot.* HELEN *is finishing her make-up. All are getting ready to go out.*)

HELEN: Thanks Amy.

AMY: Can I borrow a bit of your lippy, Helen?

HELEN: Yer.

(*Pan to window which is half open.* JOHN *and* KEVIN *are in the dark lean-to getting washed and ready to go out. They are lit from the kitchen light flooding through into lean-to. They catch sight of* AMY.)

BOTH: (*Singing*) 'Once in love with Amy! . . .'

(*Cut to:*)

INT. LEAN-TO. EARLY EVENING

Two shot from behind of JOHN *and* KEVIN *in lean-to. They are in silhouette in the foreground.* AMY *and the girls are in the bright kitchen beyond.*

AMY: (*Blushing to her roots*) Oh, I feel ashamed!

JOHN *and* KEVIN: (*Singing*) '– Always in love with Amy'

HELEN: Oh, leave her alone you two!

(*The boys laugh.*)

FRANCES: Take no notice, Amy.

JEAN: They're just letting their soft out.

[158]

JOHN *and* KEVIN: (*Singing*)
>'Her lips are much too close to mine,
>Take care my foolish heart!'

HELEN: Couple of head-the-balls!
>(*Cut to:*)

INT. KITCHEN. EARLY EVENING

Close-up (side view) of JEAN.

JEAN: Eh, Bud, will you go and get us some ciggies?
>(*Cut to:*)

INT. KITCHEN. EARLY EVENING

Medium wide shot of kitchen looking towards the door and hall, BUD *squatting on a chair left of door.*

BUD: (*Jumping off chair*) OK Jean! Throw us the money – go on! – I'll cop it.
>(*She throws the money and he catches it and runs out of the kitchen into the hall.*
>*Cut to:*)

INT. HALLWAY. EARLY EVENING

BUD *running out of kitchen. Runs into close-up, stops and screams, then slowly backs away. The girls come to the kitchen door. The lads run in from the lean-to.*

Cut to shot of a tall BLACK MAN *standing in the hall from their point of view.*

BLACK MAN: (*Speaking in a soft, gentle, polite, heavy Jamaican accent*) Is this 18 Kensington? I'm looking for Mona . . .
>(*Cut to shot of girls at kitchen door –* BUD *backs towards them. The lads move up to the camera threateningly.*)

HELEN: (*Scared*) No – it bloody well isn't. This is 18 Kensington Street. Kensington's the main road. There's no Mona here.

JOHN: (*Aggressively*) Go on! Frigg off!
>(*Cut to shot of* BLACK MAN *backing down the hall towards front door, all the time smiling.*)

BLACK MAN: (*Soft and polite*) Thank you . . . thank you . . .
>(*Cut to track and pan with girls and boys and* BUD *in tow down the dark hall to the front door.*
>*Cut to:*)

[159]

EXT. STREET. EARLY EVENING

Wide shot side view. They all come spinning out of the front door into the street – BUD *remains on the step. Track with them.*

BUD: (*Calling after them*) My Mam said don't be late.

ALL: (*Calling and waving back*) OK Bud! See yer!

(*Cut to* BUD *on the doorstep from their point of view. But closer. He waves then sits down on step, crane down with him. He sits on the step watching them go away down the street and into the night laughing and joking. Hold.*

Cut to medium close-up of BUD *in side view through cellar railings.* BUD *switches on the torch he's been carrying, first shining it into the cellar then into the night sky, as he sits on the step.*

Cut to:)

EXT. SUMMER NIGHT SKY

Shot of torchlight beam raking the night sky.

BUD: (*Voice over*) If you shine a torch into the sky – the light goes on forever.

MOTHER: (*Voice over*) Who says?

BUD: (*Voice over*) Our teacher.

(*Cut to:*)

EXT. STREET. DOORSTEP. NIGHT

Close-up of BUD *on doorstep head-on. The house and hall are dark behind him. The light from the kitchen has been switched off. He continues shining the torch into the sky then brings the torch down so that it shines directly into the camera. For a brief moment the screen goes white. Then the beam of light is taken away and we are at the far end of the hall looking down towards* BUD *at the front door. He takes the beam of light away from camera then switches the torch off. He stands at the door for a moment looking into the dark house.*

Dissolve to same angle as previous shot, although much later. The front and vestibule doors are closed and the only light in the hall is the light from the kitchen.

MOTHER: (*Voice over*) Go on up lad – I'll bring the Cocoa.

(BUD *comes out of kitchen and goes into the hall then up the dark stairs.*)

BUD: Arh – thanks Mam.
>(*A short pause then the light in the kitchen is switched off. He is followed by* MOTHER *carrying two cups of cocoa. She goes up the dark stairs. Hold on empty dark hall.* MOTHER *sings 'Me and My Shadow' in the dark.*
>*Hold. Then soundtrack:*)

BBC RADIO ANNOUNCER: 'This is the BBC Home Service. 'Lift up Your Hearts'.
>(*Dissolve/cut to:*)

INT. HALLWAY. EARLY MORNING

Long shot looking down the hall towards the front door. MOTHER *comes down the stairs and goes to the front door. She opens it and collects the milk. Looks up and down the street. The weather is cold and wet with squalls of wind and rain blowing down and across the empty street. She closes the front door and comes down the hall. She stops at the foot of the stairs.*

MOTHER: (*Calling up the stairs*) Come on you four! Make a shape! It's well past seven! (*Shivering against the cold.*) Jesus tonight – it's cold.
>(*She goes into the kitchen and switches on the light. The light floods into the grey hall.*
>*Cut to:*)

INT. PARLOUR. EARLY MORNING

Close shot of fireplace. MOTHER *puts a match to the set fire then puts a shovel against the front of the grate, then a newspaper over this for draught. Hold.*
Cut to:

INT. LEAN-TO EARLY MORNING

Close shot of MOTHER *holding a kettle beneath the cold water tap. Water splashing into kettle. Hold.*
Cut to:

INT. PARLOUR. EARLY MORNING

Close-up side view of HELEN *putting her turban on. She stands on the hearth to see in the mirror. Hold. She finishes her turban.*

Cut to:

INT. KITCHEN. EARLY MORNING

Mid wide shot from kitchen door looking into room. JOHN *is seated at the table eating his breakfast left of the gas fire. He wears only trousers and a singlet. Right of the gas fire is a bowl of water on a chair –* KEVIN *in front of the chair getting washed. He is just in his underpants.*

Cut to mid-wide shot – reverse angle of above looking towards kitchen door. KEVIN *in foreground getting washed.* BUD *comes to door and looks at* KEVIN.

KEVIN: Eh, Bud – will you do my back?

> (BUD *hesitates for a moment then comes forwards to* KEVIN. *He takes the flannel from* KEVIN *and begins to wash* KEVIN'*s back. The expression on* BUD'*s face is a sad and lonely one.*
> *Cut to:*)

INT. HALLWAY. EARLY MORNING

Three-quarter shot of KEVIN, JOHN *and* HELEN *going through the front door into the street.*

KEVIN: (*As front door opens*) God blimey! It's bleeding freezing!

> (*They go out into the street.*
> *Cut to:*)

EXT. STREET. EARLY MORNING

Side shot of KEVIN, JOHN *and* HELEN *coming out of the house. The weather is getting nastier – rain and a strong wind. They go down the street.* HELEN *crosses to other side of street and runs to work.* KEVIN *and* JOHN *bend into the wind then turn right into a side street.*

Cut to:

INT. PARLOUR. EARLY MORNING

Medium wide shot of BUD *standing in front of the fire. In front of him a bowl on chair. He is taking his pyjama-top off.*

MOTHER: (*Voice over*) I could've slept till the Lord called me this morning . . .

> (BUD *looks at her and smiles sadly.*)

MOTHER: (*Voice over*) Go on – get washed and I'll bring you your tea and toast . . .

BUD: (*Looking at her for a while – sad and lonely*) OK Mam.
 (*Slowly he begins to get washed.*
 Cut to:)

INT. PARLOUR. EARLY MORNING

Two shot side view of MOTHER *and* BUD *looking towards the parlour window. The curtains have been drawn back making everything seem grey. Mother buttons Bud's mac. Then holds his face in her hands.*
MOTHER: You'll soon be grown up, won't you lad?
 (BUD *doesn't answer. He just looks at her. Hold.*
 Cut to:)

EXT. STREET. EARLY MORNING

Wide shot of BUD *running up street to school. Squally wind and rain. Hold.*
Cut to:

EXT. SCHOOLYARD. MORNING

Pan with BUD *as he races through the empty school yard into the school. Wind and rain.*
Cut to:

INT. SCHOOL CORRIDOR. DAY

Medium long shot of BUD *coming in through door. He walks towards camera and stops at his class door. He listens for a moment then taps lightly on the door and goes in.*
Cut to:

INT. CLASSROOM. DAY

Close-up of BUD *at door. He looks both surprised and distressed. Cut to long shot from* BUD'S *point of view of empty classroom except for* MR NICHOLLS *sitting at his desk correcting exercise books. He looks up.*
MR NICHOLLS: You're late! Report to Mr Bushell, the
 Headmaster, then go upstairs to nurse in Room 10.
BUD: (*Voice over*) Yes, sir. Thank you, sir.
 (*Cut to:*)

INT. HEADMASTER'S STUDY. DAY

Mid shot of MR BUSHELL *head-on at his desk from* BUD's *point of view.*

MR BUSHELL: Why have you come?
Cut to:

INT. HEADMASTER'S STUDY. DAY

Mid shot of BUD *head-on from* MR BUSHELL's *point of view.*

BUD: Mr Nicholls told me to report late, Sir.
    (*Cut to mid-wide two shot of* BUD *and* MR BUSHELL.
    MR BUSHELL *walks into shot holding a cane.*)
MR BUSHELL: Come on.
    (BUD *lifts his hand and is caned. This time he does not cry or even*
    respond.)
MR BUSHELL: In future, be punctual.
BUD: Yes, sir. Thank you, sir.
    (*Cut to:*)

INT. ROOM 10. DAY

Mid close shot of BUD *in a line of boys which moves slowly from left to right. Pan with* BUD *as the line moves slowly.*

NURSE: (*Voice over*) Lice . . . Lice . . . Clean . . . Lice.
    (*It comes to* BUD's *turn. The nurse swirls a spatula in white*
    disinfectant and inspects his head.)
NURSE: Lice . . .
    (*He walks off camera.*)
    (*Cut:*)

INT. ROOM 10. DAY

Mid wide shot of two groups of boys. BUD *joins the group on the right – the boys with lice.*

NURSE: (*Voice over*) Clean . . . Clean . . . Lice . . .
    (*Cut to:*)

INT. ROOM 10. DAY

Close-up of BUD. *He looks at the windows – squalls of wind and rain. He is very close to tears. Pan left so that* BUD *is on edge of frame right. Soundtrack: Laughter is heard and the sound of running water. Special effects: In the space to the left of* BUD *appears the window of the kitchen which looks into the lean-to.* HELEN *is crouched over the sink and* BUD *is pouring water over her hair. Both are laughing. Pan/dissolve to:*

INT. MR NICHOLLS' CLASSROOM. DAY
Shot of MR NICHOLLS' *desk. He is marking the class register. As he calls boys' names out they answer 'Present Sir'.*
MR NICHOLLS: (*Calling the register*) Andrews, Aughton, Barnes, Bedson, Bell, Clotworthy, Crowley, Davies . . .
 (*Begin to fade his voice.*
 Cut to shot of class standing at their desks, hands joined, saying morning prayers, BUD *at the front.*)
BOYS: (*Praying*) 'Glory Be to the Father and To the Son and To the Holy Ghost.'
 (*Cut to shot of window. Outside it is raining.*)
BOYS: (*Voice over*) (*Praying*) As it was in the beginning, is now, and ever shall be, world without end. Amen.
 (*Dissolve to:*)

INT. CHURCH. LATE AFTERNOON. SUMMER SATURDAY
The icon of the face of Jesus on the cloth of St Veronica. Candles burn below it.
BUD: (*Voice over*) Jesus Mary and Joseph
 I give you my heart
 and my soul . . .
 (*Dissolve to a shot of the crucifix in the church looking along the crossbar at Christ crucified, his head droops and is turned slightly away.*)
 Jesus Mary and Joseph
 I give you my body and blood.
 (*Dissolve to shot of the high altar bathed in lighted candles and covered in flowers for quarantor.*)
 Jesus Mary and Joseph
 assist me in my last agony . . .
 (*Dissolve to two shot of* MOTHER *and* BUD *in a pew in the dark body of the church. Both are kneeling and praying.*)
 May I say when I am
 dying – Jesus mercy,
 Mary help.

[165]

(*Blessing himself*) In the name of the Father
and of the Son and of the
Holy Ghost. Amen.
(MOTHER *remains kneeling.* BUD *goes back into the pew.*
Silence.
BUD *looks at the altar for a while then at* MOTHER. *Silence.*
Soundtrack: Isabel Buchanan singing a capella, 'Ae fond kiss'.
    'Ae fond kiss and then we sever
    ae farewell alas for ever.'
Dissolve to shot of the pietà – Mary holding the dead Christ.
Soundtrack:
    'Deep in heart-wrung tears
    I'll pledge thee'
Track or pan right to left.
Dissolve to:

EXT. STREET. LATE AFTERNOON. SUMMER SATURDAY
Pan right to left to a shot of MOTHER *and* BUD *crossing the main road
and walking slowly down the street.*
Track and pan right to left.
Soundtrack:
    'Warring sighs and moans I'll wage thee'
Dissolve to:
Pan right to left to a group shot of BUD, MOTHER, HELEN, JOHN,
KEVIN *and* JEAN *and* FRANCES *sitting in and around the front door.*
MOTHER *sits on a chair just inside the front door.* BUD *stands behind
the railings. Everyone else sits on the steps. They are having an
impromptu picnic – lemonade and sandwiches.*
Soundtrack:
    'Had we never loved sae kindly
    Had we never loved sae blindly –
    Never met or never parted
    We had ne'er been broken-hearted'
Dissolve to:
Pan right to left to shot of BUD *behind railings. He gets a bottle of
lemonade from the windowsill, walks along behind the railings and
hands it to* MOTHER.
Pan/track right to left with him to her.
Soundtrack:

[166]

'Fare thee weel thou first and fairest
Fare thee weel thou best and dearest'
Dissolve to:

EXT. BUD'S HOUSE. LATE AFTERNOON. SUMMER SATURDAY
Pan right to left to two shot of FRANCES *and* KEVIN *on doorstep.*
They are laughing and talking.
Pan right to left from them.
Soundtrack: 'Thine be ilka joy and treasure.'
Dissolve and pan right to left to shot of HELEN, JEAN *and* JOHN *on*
doorstep laughing.
Soundtrack: 'Peace enjoyment love and pleasure.'
Pan right to left from them.
Dissolve to:

EXT. STREET. MAIN ROAD. LATE AFTERNOON.
SUMMER SATURDAY
Pan right to left to shot of the three school bullies bored at the top of
BUD'S *street.*
Pan from them, right to left.
Dissolve to:

EXT. BUD'S HOUSE. EARLY EVE. SUMMER SATURDAY
Pan right to left to shot of JOHN *and* JEAN *talking quietly at the*
railings then drifting down the street.
Soundtrack: 'Ae fond kiss and then we sever'.
Dissolve and pan right to left to shot of KEVIN *and* FRANCES *at*
railings. They talk softly and KEVIN *yawns.*
Soundtrack: 'Ae farewell alas for ever'.
Dissolve and pan right to left to BUD *alone at railings.*
Pan or track right to left to MOTHER *sitting inside the front door. Pan*
stops on MOTHER.
We are looking straight down the dark hall.
She gets up and takes the chair inside and disappears into kitchen.
Soundtrack: 'Deep in heart-wrung tears I'll pledge thee'.
BUD *walks into shot and goes in.*
Soundtrack: 'Warring sighs and moans I'll wage thee'.
Silence.
Hold.

[167]

Dissolve to:

INT. BUD'S HOUSE. EARLY EVENING. SUMMER SATURDAY
*Shot of·*MOTHER *from lean-to, hanging ironing on to rack. She finishes then pulls the rack up.*
Dissolve to:

INT. LEAN-TO. LATE AFTERNOON
Shot of BUD *in lean-to.*
He is listening to the rain hammering down on to the lean-to roof of doors.
He looks up then tries to touch the lean-to roof with his hand. Follow his hand.
Thundering rain.
Dissolve to:

INT. BUD'S HOUSE. NIGHT
Pitch blackness.
MOTHER, HELEN, JOHN *and* KEVIN, *holding candles below their faces, move in blackness towards camera.*
Dissolve to pitch blackness.
MOTHER, HELEN, JOHN *and* KEVIN *with candles moving up the stairs.*
Dissolve to:

INT. BUD'S HOUSE. MAIN BEDROOM. NIGHT
Pitch blackness. The light from candles on BUD'*s face.*
BUD: (*Slightly scared*) Oh, put the light on!
    (*As the light goes on a string of apples drops down in front of him.*)
    (*Recognizing the joke*) Oh, it's duck apple night!
    (*Laughter*
    Cut to:)

INT. LEAN-TO. LATE AFTERNOON
Close-up of BUD *behind lean-to window. Outside it is pouring with rain.*
Silence.
MOTHER: (*Voice over*) Come on Bud, we'll go the Hippy – Danny
    Kaye's on.

[168]

(*Cut to:*)
BULLY: (*Voice over laughing*) I thought he was Povey.
    (*Cut to:*)

INT. KITCHEN. SUMMER EVENING

Left of BUD *so that* BUD *and* HELEN *fill frame.* HELEN *bends over sink as she shampoos her hair.*
Dissolve to:

INT. LEAN-TO. SUMMER EVENING

Mid three-quarter shot from back. HELEN *bent over sink, pans of water on window sill.* BUD *standing on a chair to* HELEN'*s right.*
HELEN: OK, you can rinse it now, Bud.
    (BUD *dips his finger into one of the pans. He pulls it out very*
    quickly as the water is still too hot. He picks this pan up from the
    window sill and, giggling, pours it over HELEN'*s head.*)
HELEN: Oh, God blimey! It's scalding.
    (BUD *laughs all the more and picks up another pan and quickly*
    pours it over her head, BUD *giggling uncontrollably.*)
HELEN: You little sadist!
    (BUD *jumps down from chair and runs to kitchen.*
    Cut to:)

INT. LEAN-TO. KITCHEN WINDOW. SUMMER EVENING

Close-up of BUD.
BUD: Can we go to second house, Titch?
    (*Cut to:*)

INT. KITCHEN. SUMMER EVENING

Helen coming into close-up from BUD'*s point of view drying her hair.*
HELEN: Oh give us a chance will you? I haven't looked at the
    Echo yet – what's on?
    (*Cut to close-up of* BUD *at kitchen window.*)
BUD: Can we go and see 'Young at Heart'? It's on at the Forum.
HELEN: (*Voice over: pretending reluctance*) Oh – I suppose so.
BUD: Arh, thanks Titch!
HELEN: Go to Tyrers and get some sweets.
BUD: What sort?
HELEN: Oh – er – 'Misshapes' – the money's in me coat.

(*Pan left to right to wall then dissolve to:*)

INT. KITCHEN. LATE AFTERNOON
Pan left to right to side view mid-shot – BUD, MOTHER *and* HELEN.
They are de-lousing BUD's *hair.*
Soundtrack over dissolve and pan.
HELEN: Are you ready?
BUD: Yer!
HELEN: Well get your coat on. We don't want to miss the
    beginning do we?
    (*Cross-fade their voices.*)
BUD: (*As* HELEN *fine toothcombs his hair*) Arh! Ey, Mam!
HELEN: Keep still!
BUD: Arh, Titch!
    (*She starts to rub Lorexene into his hair.*)
BUD: Arh – it – stinks!
MOTHER: D'you prefer having nits?
BUD: No.
HELEN: Then you'll have to put up with the stink, won't you?
    (HELEN *continues combing nits out of his head.*)
MOTHER: The' are – all done.
    (*Cut to:*)

EXT. STREET. AFTERNOON
Close two shot of the backs of the heads of two boys BUD *and his friend*
ALBIE. *They are seen through the window of* 'The Only Jones's'
*barber shop. Hold. The barber beckons them and they go into the main
shop where the haircutting takes place. Crane down the window to
where it is opaque then track left to right to the door of shop.*
ALBERT DRAKE *and* BUD *come out – short back and sides.* BUD *wets
his fingers and touches* ALBIE *on the back of his neck.*
BUD: First wet Albie!
    (*They run off.*
    Cut to:)

INT. KITCHEN. LATE AFTERNOON
Shot of EDNA CLOTWORTHY, *the next-door neighbour. She is
married to* CURLY *and they have two children.* EDNA *has a good sense*

of humour but gets terribly irritated with CURLY *if he starts doing impressions of his favourite American film stars.*
She drinks tea.

HELEN: All right, Ed?

EDNA: Oh, I'm dead chokka! Cook, wash, clean – that's all I do – I never go anywhere. I'm like the bleeding Prisoner of Zenda.
(*Looks at hands.*) Look at them hands – putrid!
(*Her son* BILLY *aged eleven runs along hall and stands at kitchen door.*)

BILLY: My dad's coming, Mam.

EDNA: Tell him his tea's in the oven and I'll be in in a minute.
(*He runs off.*
Cut to close-up of MOTHER *and* BUD. *They are having their tea, gentian violet on his right ear lobe.*)

MOTHER: Little Billy isn't half going like you, isn't he?
(*Cut to medium close-up of* EDNA.)

EDNA: I know – poor little swine – I mean you could chop wood with my face, couldn't you? God Blimey what nature has in store for us.
(CURLY *appears at kitchen door.*)

CURLY: Hello, girl!

EDNA: See what I mean?
(*Cut to three shot of* MOTHER, BUD *and* HELEN. *Continue their tea.*)

HELEN: Still on the electric, Curly?

CURLY: No – I spewed it.

HELEN: Why?
(*Cut to two shot of* CURLY *and* EDNA.)

EDNA: He didn't like the fella, did he?

MOTHER: (*Voice over*) How are you managing?

CURLY: (*Beating time to a song on the chair*) I'm doing foreigners.

EDNA: Thank Christ – otherwise we'd all be eating bleeding fuse wire.
(*Cut to close-up of* MOTHER.)

MOTHER: (*Indicating* CURLY) He's full of rhythm, isn't he?
(*Cut to two shot of* EDNA *and* CURLY.)

EDNA: Yer – like St Vitus.
(CURLY *does an impression of famous Hollywood film star.*)

[171]

EDNA: (*Very irritable*) Oh don't start doing those bleeding stupid impressions!
(*Cut to close-up of* HELEN.)

HELEN: (*To* EDNA) Arh – he does them good though, doesn't he?
(*Cut to two shot of* CURLY *and* EDNA.)

EDNA: Oh God blimey Helen, don't encourage him – if he thinks he's got an audience he'll do it all the more – I'm tormented enough now.
(CURLY *does a very good impression of Edward G. Robinson.*)
(*Really annoyed.*) Who's that supposed to be?

CURLY: Edward G. Robinson.

EDNA: Sounds more like bleeding Cardew Robinson.
(*Cut to three shot of* BUD, MOTHER *and* HELEN. *They laugh. Cut to two shot of* EDNA *and* CURLY.)

EDNA: He does it just to annoy me you know. It doesn't half get on my nerves.

CURLY: Come on girl where's me scoff?

EDNA: It's in the oven – steak and onions.

CURLY: Oh, I had that last week.

EDNA: If you're not careful I'll hit you with it. Isn't it bleeding lively turning his nose up at steak and onions. Some poor bastards never get it. Oh tomorrow night it'll be dog food.

CURLY: Sounds – ruff.
(*Cut to three shot of* BUD, MOTHER *and* HELEN. *They laugh. Cut to their point of view of* EDNA.)

EDNA: (*Smiling in spite of herself*) See what I've got to put up with? I should never have married. What the bleedin' hell did I ever see in you?

BILLY: (*Voice over*) Mam!

EDNA: (*Irritated*) What!

BILLY: (*Voice over*) I'm hungry!

EDNA: (*Really irritated*) Oh – eat someone!
(EDNA *and* CURLY *get up.*)

EDNA: I'll swing for those kids one of these days. (*To* CURLY.) Come on soft ollies – we'd better go.

CURLY: (*Stopping in the doorway. To* HELEN *and* MOTHER) Have you heard the latest? They're burying Catholics in Protestant cemeteries now – they're dead like.

EDNA: (*Smiling, long-suffering*) The next bus'll be along in a few

minutes – be under it.
(*Cut to three shot of* BUD, MOTHER *and* HELEN. *They laugh.*)
MOTHER: See you, Ed.
HELEN: T'ra, Curly!
(*Cut to:*)

INT. HALLWAY/KITCHEN. EARLY EVENING
Two shot back view of CURLY *followed by* EDNA *going down hall.*
EDNA: ⎫
CURLY: ⎬ See yer! T'ra.
EDNA: You need a shave.
CURLY: So do you.
(*Both laugh.*)
EDNA: Oh stop messing! Tant!
(*Cut to:*)

INT. KITCHEN. EARLY EVENING
Special effects: Three shot side view of MOTHER, BUD *and* HELEN
finishing their tea.
Pan right to left so that this group is on the edge of frame right. In the
space left of them BUD *comes through the clinic doors.*
Pan or dissolve to:

INT. SCHOOL CLINIC. MORNING
Shot of BUD *coming through the double doors of the school clinic. He*
comes into close-up and stops. He has gentian violet where his right
earlobe meets his cheek. He stands in the silence. Hold.
Cut to: very wide shot of school clinic. It seems large and bare to BUD.
Eau de nil walls and brown lino. Right of frame the treatment cubicle
inside which a NURSE *moves. Left of frame a large highly polished*
refectory table. At the far end of it sits the NURSE *who was inspecting*
the boys for lice. BUD *walks into shot frame right and walks to the*
table and stops half-way down it, a few feet away from the NURSE.
Silence as she writes, taking no notice of him. Hold.
Cut to mid-shot of NURSE. BUD's *point of view; she is about fifty,*
bespectacled and intensely clean. White and all ice. Her voice is soft
and cool. Pause.
NURSE: (*Without ever looking at him*) Your card.
(*Cut to mid-shot of* BUD *from* NURSE's *point of view. He puts*

the card on the table and just looks at her. Hold. Silence.
Cut to BUD'*s point of view of* NURSE.)

NURSE: (*Looking at his card*) Is it your ear again?
(*He doesn't answer.*)
I suppose you've been picking at it, haven't you?
(*Cut to* NURSE'*s point of view of* BUD. *He's too afraid to reply.*
He just stands there.)
(*Voice over*) What nasty little creatures you little boys are.
(*Cut to:*)

EXT. SCHOOL PLAYGROUND. MORNING
Close shot of the three bullies dragging and punching BUD *into a*
secluded part of the school yard. Track quickly with them right to
left. The whistle is heard. All activity stops.
THIRD BOY: (*To* BUD) If you snitch we'll get you tonight!
(*Cut to:*)

INT. MR NICHOLLS' CLASSROOM. MORNING
Medium wide shot of MR NICHOLLS *head-on at his desk. He is*
taking the geography lesson.
MR NICHOLLS: (*Dictating from a textbook*) 'The Process of
Erosion. Erosion is the cumulative effect of a great variety
of processes . . .'
(*Cut to medium wide shot of classroom from* MR NICHOLLS'
point of view, head-on. BUD *at the front desk of the second row.*
All the boys write quickly as MR NICHOLLS *continues to*
dictate.)
MR NICHOLLS: (*Voice over*) '. . . in general these can be divided
into five groups . . .'
(*Cut to close-up of* MR NICHOLLS. *Pan with him right to left to*
blackboard at window.)
MR NICHOLLS: (*Reads off blackboard*) '. . . 1. River Erosion.
2. Rain Erosion.
3. Glacial Erosion.
4. Wind Erosion.
and
5. Marine Erosion.'
(*Cut to close-up of* BUD *at desk writing, head-on.*)
(*Voice over*) '. . . life also co-operates in the work of

destruction. 1. Rivers and their valleys . . .'
(*Cut to:*)

INT. SWIMMING BATHS. MORNING

*Close shot of the wooden doors of the cubicles running down the entire
length of the pool. Suddenly the hand of the games master bangs open
a door.* BUD *half dressed, is startled and embarrassed.*

GAMES MASTER: Come on! Hurry up! We all know what you're
trying to hide!

(*The rest of the doors open and boys come out.*

*Cut to close shot of the water in the pool. Bodies splashing into
and out of the water.* BUD *comes wading gingerly into shot –
scared of the water. Suddenly someone from beneath the water
takes* BUD's *legs from under him. He falls backwards into the
water – terrified. Hold for a moment – all natural sound fades.
Then crane down and over the placid surface of the pool. The
water gently lapping.*)

Soundtrack (*over and through dissolve*): *all in the pub singing*
'Slow Boat to China'.

(*Dissolve to:*)

EXT. STREET PUB. NIGHT

Continue crane down.

Soundtrack of 'Slow Boat to China'.

Continue crane down to mid-wide shot of BUD, *back to camera,
looking towards the pub.* BUD *stands centre frame in front of the pub
door which is flanked by two large ornate windows. The pub is an
ornate victorian one – marble facings and elaborate carved, frosted
glass windows, which read* 'Ind Coope Traditional Ales' 'Fine
Wines and Spirits'. *People drift in and out.*

Soundtrack of the singing continues.

Applause, laughter.

BUD *walks towards the pub door. Track in on it with him and past
him into back parlour.*

JOHN: (*Voice over doing a very bad impression of Jack Palance*)
Who's this Curly? 'I am Attila-Attila the Hun'.

CURLY: (*Voice over*) Esther Williams.

(*Laughter.*)

JOHN: (*Voice over*) You bastard!

[175]

KEVIN: (*Voice over*) Eh, Edna tell him to behave will you?

EDNA: (*Voice over*) I know – people have been strangled for less haven't they?

>(*By now* EDNA *and* CURLY *and all Bud's family can be seen at an end table near the door leading to the toilets. Continue tracking towards toilets.*)

CURLY: (*To* EDNA *who gets up*) Want a drink girl?

EDNA: In a minute – I'm just going for a twinkle.

CURLY: Say one for me.

EDNA: Oh, shut it!

>(*She goes into the ladies' toilet. Continue track into the darkness. Hold on darkness.*
>*Dissolve to:*)

INT. HALL. BUD'S HOUSE. NIGHT

Hold on darkness of the lean-to. Then track back into hall. EDNA *comes through the door leading from the lean-to.*

EDNA: (*To* BUD – *putting her cold hands on either side of his face*) It's perishing out there!

>(BUD *squeals and giggles. He runs and sits on the stairs.* EDNA *stops at the kitchen door.*)

CURLY: (*Singing and tipsy*) 'Civilization! Bongo! Bongo! Bongo!'

EDNA: (*Smiling in spite of herself*) Isn't that singing bleeding terrible? Like an ollie in a bottle.

>(*Cut to:*)

INT. HALL. BUD'S HOUSE. NIGHT

Shot looking up the hall towards CURLY *who is standing with* JOHN *and* KEVIN *in front of the open vestibule – by the parlour.*
CURLY *carries on singing.*

EDNA: (*Voice over*) Oh, choke him, somebody!

>(*Cut to mid-wide shot of* CURLY's *point of view of* BUD – *amidst all the girls – on the stairs.* EDNA *is framed right at foot of stairs.*)

JEAN: (*To* CURLY) Now, Curly, behave yourself! Otherwise Edna'll give you forty lashes.

EDNA: (*To* CURLY) That'd be an incentive wouldn't it love?

>(*Cut to shot looking up hall towards* CURLY. JOHN *and* KEVIN *go into parlour.*)

[176]

JOHN: (*To* CURLY) Have you got a bevvy Curly?

CURLY: You're all right, John, me Judy'll get me up one.
(*Cut to group shot with* EDNA *at the foot of the stairs.*)

EDNA: You've had enough. You can't have just one drink, you've got to get pallatic.
(*Cut to shot of* CURLY *by parlour door.*)

CURLY: (*Even tipsier – one too many*) Arh, go on girl – be nice nice to be nice – (*To himself*) People are people –
(*Cut to group shot with* EDNA *in close-up.*)

EDNA: Well they're not grapefruit are they? (*To girls*) God help him. He's in a world of his own.
(*Cut to mid-wide shot of* CURLY *at parlour door.* CURLY *does another impression.* EDNA *enters shot.*)
(*Irritated*) And don't start doing those stupid bleeding impressions – otherwise wooden overcoat – savvy?

CURLY: (*As Edward G. Robinson*) See here kid –!

EDNA: (*Pushing him into parlour, really annoyed*) Oh shut up! Bleeding screwball!
(*Cut to:*)

INT. PARLOUR. BUD'S HOUSE. NIGHT

Medium close-up two shot of EDNA *and* CURLY. *She sits in a chair and he sits on the arm to her left.*

CURLY *sings 'When I Leave the World Behind'.*

(*Laughter.*)

(*Half-way through the first verse,* EDNA *begins to cry and* CURLY *slips his arm around her shoulder.* CURLY *sings second verse. All join in the chorus.*)

EDNA: (*Through tears*) That was my Mam's song, that.

CURLY: (*Hugging her*) Come on girl – you give us one.
(EDNA *sings 'I Don't Know Why I Just Do'.*
She gestures everyone to join in and they do so. Pan around room left to right past JOHN, KEVIN, JEAN, FRANCES, AMY *then finish on* MOTHER *in close-up by the fire.*
All join in the song.
Applause.)

MOTHER: Come on – our Bud now!
(*Cut to wide shot – looking at the curtain which serves as a door for the parlour.*

[177]

A guest draws the curtain back to camera left and BUD *and*
HELEN *come in, singing 'A Couple of Swells'.*
Big finish. Curtain drops. Applause.
Cut to:)

EXT. STREET OUTSIDE BUD'S HOUSE. NIGHT
Medium close-up head-on from outside of BUD *and* HELEN *at the open*
parlour window – they lean out and look to their right towards the
front door. Pan from them right to left.

CURLY: (*Voice over*) Well you're always saying I never take you
anywhere . . .
(CURLY *and* EDNA *come out of the front door and into the street.*
Pan with them.)

CURLY: . . . We'll go the Dance.

EDNA: The Grafton's for bits of kids – we're too old.
(*Continue panning with them as they walk in front of the parlour*
window.)

CURLY: You're as old as you feel.

EDNA: Look – you may think you're Peter Pan but I'm not
bleeding Wendy. (*Determined.*) We're not going!

CURLY: (*Stopping in front of the parlour window*) Yes Edna. No
Edna. Three bags full Edna. (*Suddenly realizing he has no*
jacket on.) Eh, where's me jacket? It's cold.
(EDNA *trying to put his arms in the armholes.*)
Eh, what's happening?

EDNA: Get your arms in!

CURLY: My tiny hand is frozen.

EDNA: If it was any bigger it'd have frost-bite.

CURLY: (*Singing*) 'Oh you beautiful doll!
You great big beautiful doll . . .!'
(*Walks off frame left.*)

EDNA: Whatever you do, Helen, don't get married – you could
end up with someone like this soft bastard –
(CURLY *continues to sing.*)
(*Walks after him*) Oh button it!

CURLY: (*Singing fades.*)
(*Cut to medium close-up head-on of* BUD *and* HELEN *at open*
window. They wave their good nights to EDNA *and* CURLY *then*
HELEN *disappears back into parlour.* BUD *stays at the window*

looking into the sky then down into the dark cellar.
Pan down away from window and crane over the cellar steps and
railings to the street. The railings are reflected on the pavement,
splayed out. Hold.
Dissolve to:)

EXT. STREET. DAY

Same camera position as above.
Sunday morning. Bright sunshine. Church bells.
Crane down to street level to two shot of BUD *and his friend* ALBIE
standing on the cellar steps looking out through the railings. They seem
fascinated by something.
Cut to close-up of a man walking by on the opposite side of the street. He
looks completely emaciated, his face and neck eaten away. He looks
weary from pain. He seems to glide and drift painfully by.
ALBIE: (*Voice over*) That's Mr Yates.

> (*Cut to two shot head-on of* ALBIE *and* BUD. *They move away*
> *from the railings and sit down on the cellar steps.*)

ALBIE: (*Quietly*) He's got cancer.

> (*Silence.*)

MOTHER: Come on Bud! Time for Mass.
BUD: OK, Mam! See you after, Albie.
ALBIE: OK.

> (*They run up the steps.*
> *Cut to:*)

INT. KITCHEN. DAY

Medium-wide shot of an upturned bike – resting on two chairs – fills the
screen. KEVIN *– just wearing dungarees is centre frame.* BUD *is seen*
behind the wheel frame right. He is bored. KEVIN *mends a puncture.*
BUD: Are you going to Cast Iron Shore, Kev?
KEVIN: No. Woolton Woods.
BUD: Can I come with you?
KEVIN: You haven't got a bike, Bud lad.

> (*Silence.*)

BUD: Will you bring us some pears back, Kev?
KEVIN: Yer.

> (*Silence.* KEVIN *takes a drink from a bottle of Double Diamond.*)

BUD: Can I have some of your drink, Kev?

[179]

KEVIN: You won't like it.
>   (BUD *drinks and makes a face.*)
BUD: Arh, it's horrible!
KEVIN: (*Laughing*) I told you you wouldn't like it.
>   (KEVIN *finishes and turns the pedals of the bike. The wheels spin
>   and* BUD *is obliterated by them.*
>   *Cut to:*)

EXT. STREET. DAY

Sunday afternoon – bright sunshine.
Close-up of BUD *on doorstep, bored and lonely.*
BUD: Can't I come with you? Arh, go on! Let me!
>   (*Cut to wide shot from* BUD'*s point of view of* FRANCES, JOHN,
>   KEVIN, JEAN, HELEN *and some others, all on bikes. The group
>   cycle up the street.*
>   *Track with them. They disappear into the main road.*)
BUD: (*Voice over, calling after them*) Don't forget the pears!
>   (*Cut to close-up three-quarter side view of* BUD *on doorstep
>   looking up the empty street. He walks down the step. Pan with
>   him left to right as he trails his hand along the railings.*
>   *Soundtrack:*
>   BBC Radio's Rays A Laugh. *A last joke is heard. Laughter.
>   Applause.*)
BBC RADIO ANNOUNCER: 'That was *Rays a Laugh* starring Ted
>   Ray with Kitty Bluett, Kenneth Connor, Laidman Brown,
>   Rosalind Knight, and Pat Coombes . . .'
>   (*Fade sound.* BUD *gets to the top of the cellar steps and stops.
>   There is an iron bar which runs from just below the window sill to
>   the railings. He looks at this bar for a moment then jumps.*
>   *Dissolve to shot directly overhead of the cellar steps.* BUD *swings
>   on the bar. Hold.*
>   *Soundtrack: the passing bell is heard.*
>   *Then still directly overhead crane and track away right to left
>   from swinging* BUD.
>   *Dissolve to:*)

INT. MR NICHOLLS' CLASSROOM. AFTERNOON

Continue craning and tracking right to left still directly overhead.
MR NICHOLLS: Get into line.

[180]

(The boys do so.)
Turn.
(The boys do so.)
Good night, boys.
BOYS: Good night, Sir.
MR NICHOLLS: Off you go.
(Soundtrack: Terry Thomas's voice over from 'Private's Progress'.
The boys snake out. Continue craning and tracking directly overhead – right to left.
Dissolve to:)

INT. CINEMA. NIGHT

Continue craning and tracking right to left directly overhead.
The projection light flickers over the heads of a full cinema audience.
MOTHER *and* BUD *walk down the aisle and take seats at the end of the row. The aisle runs down centre of frame. Continue craning and tracking.*
Soundtrack: Debbie Reynolds singing the title song 'Tammy' from the film Tammy and the Bachelor.
Dissolve to:

INT. CHURCH. DAY

Continue craning and tracking right to left directly overhead. The church is full. The congregation standing. The altar bell is rung three times. The congregation sinks to its knees.
CONGREGATION:
Holy! Holy! Holy!
Lord God of Hosts!
Heaven and Earth are full of thy Glory!
(Continue craning and tracking.
Priest comes into shot. He elevates the host. The altar bell rings three times.
Dissolve to:)

EXT. STREET. DAY

Continue craning and tracking right to left down street directly overhead. Crane and track comes to rest when the pavement and cellar outside Bud's house is reached.

[181]

ALBIE *and another boy enter shot.*
Cut to close-up of BUD *head-on leaning out of front bedroom window watching* ALBIE *and another boy walk up street.*
Cut to:

INT. FRONT BEDROOM. DAY
Three-quarter back view of BUD *rushing from window to downstairs. Pan with him left to right.*
Cut to:

INT. HALLWAY. DAY
Shot of BUD *rushing downstairs and to front door. Pan with him right to left. He stops at the front door.*
Cut to:

EXT. STREET AND FRONT DOOR. DAY
Close-up of BUD *at door. He looks up the street after* ALBIE *and then looks crestfallen.*
Cut to:

EXT. STREET. DAY
Shot of ALBIE *and other boy disappearing down street from* BUD's *point of view.*
Cut to:

INT. HALLWAY. DAY
Long shot of BUD *at the front door. He comes down the hall towards camera and into close-up – very dejected. He stops at kitchen door and looks towards his* MOTHER.
Cut to:

INT. KITCHEN. DAY
Close-up side view of MOTHER *at kitchen table rolling pastry. She is humming to herself. Silence.*
MOTHER: (*To* BUD) Aren't you going to the pictures?
   (*Cut to:*)

INT. HALLWAY. DAY
Close-up of BUD – MOTHER's *point of view.*

[182]

BUD: I've got no one to go with.
   (*Cut to:*)

   INT. KITCHEN. DAY
Close-up side view of MOTHER – BUD's *point of view.*
MOTHER: What about Albie?
   (*Cut to:*)

   INT. HALLWAY. DAY
Close-up of BUD – MOTHER's *point of view.*
BUD: He's just gone past with John Hughes.
   (*Cut to:*)

   INT. KITCHEN. DAY
Close-up (side view) of MOTHER – BUD's *point of view.*
MOTHER: Why don't you run after them and ask can you go with
   them?
   (*Cut to:*)

   INT. HALLWAY. DAY
Close-up of BUD – MOTHER's *point of view. He shakes his head.*
Hold.
Cut to:

   INT. KITCHEN. DAY
Close-up of MOTHER – BUD's *point of view. She continues rolling*
pastry and humming softly to herself. Hold.
Cut to:

   INT. HALLWAY. DAY
Shot looking directly up the hall towards the front door. BUD *drifts*
towards the front door. He stops at it for a while then drifts into the
street.
Cut to:

   EXT. STREET. LATE AFTERNOON
Low-angle shot of BUD *behind cellar railings. He looks up the street.*
Cut to BUD's *point of view. Low-angle shot of a coal cart being pulled*
by a horse. The horse and cart stop outside BUD's *house. The coalman*

*jumps down and secures the horse. He jumps back upon the cart to
select a bag of coal for delivery.*
Cut to:

INT. CELLAR. LATE AFTERNOON
*Wide shot of coal-hole (right of frame), cellar door (centre frame) and
cellar window (left of frame): through it* BUD *can be seen.*
BUD *moves away from the railings and moves down the cellar steps
towards the cellar door – which is closed.*
*Special effects: the coalman lifts up the iron lid which covers the
coal-hole. Simultaneously the cellar door opens of its own accord. A
shaft of conical light comes pouring through the coal-hole.* BUD *just
stands there – trance-like – looking into the quiet, dark cellar. Then the
coalman delivers a rush of coal. Black dust billows out of the coal-
hole, the sound of the unloading coal getting louder and louder and
huge black clouds of coal dust gradually filling the cellar.* BUD
continues just to stand there.
*Through the coal dust the shaft of light is just discernible then the
coal-hole lid is slammed back on – like a door shutting – a tomb.*
BUD *continues to stand there – terrified – as black coal dust silently fills
the silent, dark cellar.*
Soundtrack: Jean Simmons' voice over from Great Expectations.
　　'He's just a boy. A common labouring boy . . .'
　　(BUD *starts coming into the cellar towards the camera. He is
　　crying uncontrollably. He moves past the camera.*
　　Dissolve to:)

EXT. CELLAR. LATE AFTERNOON
Wide shot of cellar from cellar door.
BUD, *his back to camera, looking into, being consumed by, the black
coaldust. He disappears from view. Silence. The coaldust is still
billowing out.*
Soundtrack: Martita Hunt's voice over from Great Expectations.
BUD: (*Voice over, crying uncontrollably*) Mam! Mam! It's dark in
　　here!
　　(*His crying fades.*
　　Soundtrack: laughter is heard from decades ago.
　　It fades. Silence.
　　The black clouds of coaldust begin to disperse and the cellar is

[184]

empty and quiet and derelict. It is now night. Plaster and powder fall, then all is silence. Then pan around to cellar door and crane up – simultaneously – through the derelict house.
Soundtrack:)

BUD: (*Voice over*) What did you get for Christmas, Albie?

ALBIE: (*Voice over*) A cowie outfit and a Bren gun.

BUD: (*Voice over*) Our Kevin bought me a watch.

(*As crane rises to front door level, everywhere is derelict.*
BUD *and* ALBIE *are seated on the front step, their backs to camera, and are in silhouette. They are shining their torches up into the night sky. They are silent with just the torchlight. Crane past them to the sky along the line of the torchlight. The light from the torches raking the night sky – a sky full of sudden clouds and crystal clear dark blue/black.*)

BUD: (*Voice over*) Some of those stars are dead – the light from them started out when Jesus was alive . . .
(*Pause.*)

ALBIE: (*Voice over*) How d'you know?

BUD: (*Voice over*) Our teacher said . . .
(*Crane comes to rest on a wide shot of the night sky.*)
Soundtrack: the crackle of radio waves heard from deep space.)

TEACHER: (*Voice over, still dictating*) '4. Wind Erosion. The waters of the seas readily respond by movement to the brushing of the wind over the surface; to the variations of temperature and salinity; to the gravitational attraction of the moon and sun and to the coriolis force. A. Tides and Currents . . .'
(*Fade his voice.*
Soundtrack: his voice fades back into the crackle of radio waves heard from deep space. The torches continue to rake the night sky. Hold on sky.
Soundtrack:)

MOTHER: (*Voice over*) Come on lad! Down the Red Lane!

BUD: (*Voice over*) OK, Mam.

HELEN, JOHN, KEVIN: (*Voice over*) Happy Christmas, Bud.

MOTHER: (*Voice over*) Happy Christmas, lad.

BUD: (*Voice over*) Happy Christmas, Mam.
(*The torchlight fades.*

Soundtrack: the radio waves crackling fades.
Hold on sky. Some white clouds scud across the night sky. All is
silence. Then soundtrack: a four-part choir singing a cappella,
'The Long Day Closes' by Arthur Sullivan.)

    'No star is o'er the lake
    Its pale watch keeping
    The moon is half awake
    Through gray mist creeping
    The last red leaves fall round
    The porch of roses
    The clock has ceased to sound
    The long day closes . . .'
(Hold on sky. The sky continues to change.
Soundtrack:)

    'Sit by the silent hearth
      In calm endeavour
    To count the sounds of mirth
      Now dumb forever
    Heed not how hope believes
      And fate disposes
    Shadow is around the eaves
    The long day closes . . . '
(Hold on sky. The sky continues to change.
Soundtrack:)

CHOIR: 'The lighted windows dim
      Are fading slowly
    The fire that was so trim
      Now quivers lowly
    Go to the dreamless bed
      Where grief reposes
    Thy book of toil is read
    The long day closes . . .'
(Hold on the sky. It continues to change.
Soundtrack:)

CHOIR: 'Go to the dreamless bed
      Where grief reposes
    Thy book of toil is read
    Thy book of toil is read
    Go to the dreamless bed

The long day closes.'
(*The radio waves are heard from deep space.*
Fade to black.)

New Faber Screenplays

My Beautiful Laundrette with *The Rainbow Sign*
The most popular British film of the eighties, together with Hanif
Kureishi's extended autobiographical essay about growing up in a
racist society.

Sex, Lies and Videotape
How did a first-time director get to win the most coveted prize in
the film industry, the Palme d'Or at Cannes? Steven Soderbergh
explains how, together with the screenplay that launched his
career.

Decalogue (including *A Short Film About Killing* and
A Short Film About Love)
Krzysztof Kieślowski's remarkable sequence of films based on the
Ten Commandments also includes an Introduction by Kieślowski
about his career and a Foreword by Stanley Kubrick.

Barton Fink and *Miller's Crossing*
Another winner from Cannes, this time an unprecedented win of
Best Actor, Best Direction and Best Film, all for *Barton Fink* in
1991. An automatic classic, along with the Coen Brothers'
previous success, *Miller's Crossing*.

Faber Classic Screenplays

THE BATTLESHIP POTEMKIN Sergei Eisenstein
THREE FILMS OF W. C. FIELDS: *Never Give a Sucker an Even
Break*, *Tillie and Gus*, *The Bank Dick*.
NAPOLEON Abel Gance
THE THIRD MAN Graham Greene
MASTERWORKS OF THE BRITISH CINEMA: *The Lady Vanishes*,
Brief Encounter, *Henry V*
GONE WITH THE WIND Sidney Howard
SEVEN SAMURAI AND OTHER SCREENPLAYS Akira Kurosawa
METROPOLIS Fritz Lang
THE WIZARD OF OZ Edgar Allen Woolf

THE SERVANT AND OTHER SCREENPLAYS Harold Pinter
ON THE WATERFRONT Budd Schulberg
ANDREI RUBLEV Andrei Tarkovsky
JULES ET JIM François Truffaut
GREED Eric von Stroheim

Coming Soon to a Bookshop Near You . . .

Malle on Malle
In the latest in our successful series of film directors discussing
their own work and careers, Louis Malle looks back over his life
and work. Edited by Philip French.

Patty di Phusa and Other Writings Pedro Almódovar
Hilarious and risqué short stories plus personal writings on film
from the most popular Spanish film director in the world!

The French Brothers' Wild and Crazy Film Quiz Book
Quite simply the best film quiz book – ever.

If you would like a complete Faber Film Books stocklist, then
please write to:

Promotions Department
Faber and Faber Ltd
3 Queen Square
London WCIN 3AU